SPIRITUAL DYSLEXIA
THE AWAKENING

Duane C. McDermott

Copyright © 2025 by Duane C. McDermott

All rights reserved. This book or any portion thereof may not be reproduced or used in any manner whatsoever without the express written permission of the publisher except for the use of brief quotations in a book review.

Printed in the United States of America

ISBN 978-1-7354642-6-8

Contact the author at mrduane.mcdermott@gmail.com

All scriptures came from the King James Black Heritage Edition, World Copyright 1976, Today, Inc.

DEDICATION

To Meva L. McDermott, my beloved mother:

Your unwavering faith, wisdom, and love have been the foundation of my spiritual journey. Through your prayers, guidance, and steadfast trust in God, you have taught me to see with the eyes of faith, even when life's path seemed unclear.

CONTENTS

Introduction...vii

Chapter 1 The Holy Spirit.............................1

Chapter 2 The Foolishness of Preaching................17

Chapter 3 Job..29

Chapter 4 Heritage...................................41

Chapter 5 Born Again.................................53

Chapter 6 Gods Unlimited Resources!..................67

Chapter 7 The Seven Churches of Revelation...........85

About the Author......................................97

INTRODUCTION

Spiritual dyslexia is a difficulty in comprehending biblical spiritual insights when reading from Genesis to Revelation. Many believers start with a great zeal to read the bible but find themselves frustrated because of the lack of understanding. It is impossible to overcome spiritual dyslexia without the help of the Holy Spirit. People have used religious indoctrination to train new converts for a long time, but this method has proven unsuccessful in creating a Godly influenced education. The major difference between religious indoctrination and spiritual education is that spiritual education unlocks the mind universally in God, while religious indoctrination locks the mind to a set of beliefs without questioning them. Religious teaching establishes unwavering beliefs as absolute facts. In other words, man's religion has done more harm than good when it comes to knowing who you are in the heart and mind of God. Spiritual Dyslexia does not differ from the clinical definition of human dyslexia, defined as a learning disorder that involves difficulty in learning to read or interpret words, letters, and symbols without affecting a person's general intelligence. We should read the Bible according to the customary rules of literal grammar; however, we cannot overlook the fact that the

Bible also speaks figuratively and symbolically. As the author of Spiritual Dyslexia, my prayer and hope is to help you dispel the dogmatic, systematic teachings of man, while becoming more spiritually enlightened as you read the pages of this book.

Duane C. McDermott

CHAPTER 1

THE HOLY SPIRIT

On that great and terrible day, Jesus spoke his last seven words, which have been repeated throughout the history of the church during the Passover celebration. On that dreadful day, his disciple watched in horror as a Roman guard pierced him in his side, and then out came water and blood. As the people gathered around the foot of the cross, Christ said; it is finished, Father into your hands I commend my spirit! Now, the Spirit of Christ is available for anyone who would receive him. This is the comforter that was promised to the disciples of Christ and has been freely given to all believers of Christ. The Holy Spirit is not this force of energy that we catch from time to time, but He is the indwelling power of God that leads man in all righteousness. There is nothing religious about the Holy Spirit other than He only leads humanity to Christ for the remission of sin.

The primary work of the Holy Spirit will never work outside of the body of Christ. Because the world system is subject to Satan's power, the natural man cannot receive spiritual things from God. 1 Corinthians 2: 7-16. The believers of Christ must fully understand that faith does not come from the wisdom of man, but is rooted deeply in the word of God. The Holy Spirit gives utterance, leading us into the wisdom of God. This wisdom that I speak about is not based on the wisdom of what world leaders teach but is only manifested in the body of Christ by men and women who have been called to teach the word of God by comparing spiritual things with spiritual things. When a person receives Christ as lord and savior, they become overshadowed by the power of the Holy Spirit, which becomes their sixth sense.

This Holy Spirit was in Adam but had totally vanished from the thoughts of man by the time of Noah. Genesis 6 clearly states that God's Spirit won't always remain with humanity because of our sinful nature. God's spirit is evident throughout biblical history, fully revealed in Christ's baptism and released upon the world through his crucifixion. The Spirit of Christ is sometimes called the Holy Ghost, which is an unseen force of energy that can fill a body, room, or space and change the atmosphere in which it fills. The Bible teaches that God, in his purest form, is an unseen force of energy, and worship must be done in spirit and truth. (John 4:24)

God is the eternal light energy, and he has created everything seen and unseen. We cannot measure or calculate light; therefore, we cannot contain it. Most relate to God through his creations, but God's Spirit transcends creation, entering his predestined counsel. Everything in existence is predetermined, which is what God's predestined counsel means. The Holy Spirit reveals God's predestined counsel to humanity. According to Isaiah 6:1-13, the Holy Spirit empowers blood-covered saints, granting them authority to enter God's throne room. The Holy Spirit, Christ Jesus, and Eternal Father have always, and will always, sit on the Throne of Heaven as one being. When you receive the gift of the Holy Spirit, he will give you the power to judge both earthly things and heavenly things. The Spirit of God will stir your emotions, preventing you from losing control in a fit of rage and uncontrollable action that can lead to bodily harm. On the other hand, evil spirits of divination can possess a human body when there are unconfessed sins of inner commotion, confusion, or conflicts of the soul. When the Holy Spirit reveals truth, stirring up awareness of sin, demonic forces oppose God's work within a person, leading to intense emotional turmoil. This took place when Jesus met the naked man at the tomb and confronted the demons in his life. When the demons saw Christ, they began to cry out because they feared being tormented, knowing that this was their demise for all eternity. Jesus cast the demons into a herd of swine, which ran off a cliff and killed themselves, which released these demonic spirits back into the spirit realm of eternal darkness. (Mark 5:1-20) In Babel, the sacrifice of the firstborn male child to the fire god caused the slain children's families to suffer uncontrollable fits of rage because of tormented souls.

The Holy Spirit is Christ in spirit form, so the scripture will refer to the Spirit as He and not it. (1 John 5:7). Christ would often testify that he could do nothing without the Father, and he also testified when you see him, you have seen the Father referring to his oneness with the Father. In the quest to understand the work and operation of the Holy Spirit, one's heart must be totally surrendered to Christ. This means that we must expose every dark area in our lives to the light of Christ, which grants forgiveness for sin. This light and darkness cannot house the same space at the same time, so darkness must flee in the presence of light. The Scripture starts with the transformational work of God when God said let there be light, and the dark, void, formless earth began to restore, reconstruct, and repair itself to its original created purpose. When the enlightenment of Christ takes place in the life of a believer, we become renewed, repaired, and reconstructed in this same process, which transforms us back to the original state of spirit. Confession of sin is the only way to get the attention of the spirit of God.

In the Gospels, there is a story that Jesus told his disciples concerning two men who went to the temple to pray. One was a self-righteous Pharisee, and the other was a conniving tax collector who knew that inwardly, he had been immoral in his dealings with himself and others and was guilty of sin. The Pharisees stood up and prayed: "God, I thank thee, that I am not as other men are, extortioners, unjust, adulterers, or even as this publican." Then the tax collector stood at a distance and would not even look up to the heavens, but he beat on his chest saying lord have mercy on me for I am a sinner. Jesus concludes his story by saying to his disciples that the man who confessed his sins before God went home justified before God. For all those who exalt themselves will be humbled, and those who humble themselves and confess their brokenness will be exalted. (Luke 18: 10-14) This parable was given to remind the believer that self-righteousness is not an act of the Holy Spirit. The Holy Spirit teaches the believers of God to search their hearts for all unrighteousness, and he promises to restore those infected areas of sin with love, grace, and forgiveness, which will make the wounded whole again. The truth of the matter is the spirit already has knowledge of what you need before you ask, but will only meet your need based on your personal request unto him.

In the modern church, people know this divine connection as the devotion period, when they offer prayers for believers and non-believers of Christ to obtain forgiveness for their sins. This is the most important time of the worship service because it is the time when the ushering in of God's spirit fills the room and the physical bodies of the people. This was demonstrated on the day of Pentecost, as the disciples were praying. A mighty wind filled the upper room, and the people began to speak with a cloven tongue. Throughout scripture, the Holy Spirit has moved as a great force of wind, which was seen when the Red Sea was parted for Moses. The Holy Spirit also moved as a supernatural field of energy when he split the walls of Jericho. The Spirit of God is all powerful, and can control all natural elements, such as the fire in Moses' burning bush, and just as powerful when he speaks to the believer in a small, still voice as he spoke to Elijah while hiding in a cave from Jezebel. There are many claims of spiritual enlightenment from all the world's religions, but it's only in Christ that we have been able to witness resurrection power over the grave. All religious ideas may have a form of godliness but deny the power of Christ, who is the incarnation of the Spirit of God. We should discredit no one's freedom to have their religious belief based on historical or cultural development but share the principle teachings of Christ. Christ is the foundation and chief cornerstone that the builder has rejected! (Psalms 118:22) The Spirit of God testifies and witnesses of Christ in the Old and New Testament with a divine revelation of the spiritual world to come.

The spirit searches the deep things of God. (1 Corinthians 2: 9-10) The transformation process of the Holy Spirit only works from the inside out, and there is no way to manipulate the process. The Holy Spirit is guided only by the truth and will act accordingly. Holy Scripture is divinely inspired; thus, interpreting it privately without respecting God's Spirit is wrong. The Bible has been one of the most read books in history and one of the most misunderstood books known to carnal minded man. The Bible often ends scripture with; he that has an ear, let them hear, which is directly associated with the inner ear of the spirit. When mankind tries to read and understand the scripture based solely on systemic theology, morals, principles, history, or science, there will be errors in the interpretation because the bible is first based on revelation, not information. Therefore, an atheist can study the word of God and its information, but receive no revelation because there is no inspiration. The prophetic word can be misinterpreted when men don't use the word of God as the guideline of truth. This mishandling of God's word has led to domination and division

Spiritual Dyslexia

based on private interpretations. Diversity is not division, and unity is not uniformity, so we all have the right and free will to worship the universal Creator in spirit and truth. The foundation of all spiritual enlightenment begins, and ends with Christ as the pathway to the throne room of God, so without Christ, there is no way to gain access. If you haven't yet accepted Christ as your path to God's Kingdom, I urge you to do so now. We're entering the spiritual realm, and without divine protection, you'll be vulnerable to enemy attacks. AMEN.

When moving from the physical world to the spiritual world, we understand we are moving into a higher level of conscience that will lead us into a different dimension of the inner workings of the brain. This process can only be achieved by totally detaching yourself from any and every material asset. As you become one with your spirit, you will connect to the eternal spirit of God. The spirit reveals all things that are hidden behind the veil that separates the natural and supernatural realms. Beyond the veil, there are four descriptive beings which are the Father, Son, Holy Spirit, and Satan. When transcending into the third dimension of heaven, we reach our highest level of conscious awareness, which is 100 percent spirit, so the flesh cannot enter in. In the Spirit realm there is nothing material there, so everything that appears; appears by things that do not appear. (Hebrews 11:3)

Many people use spirits of divination, which are evil spirits, to transfer over into the spirit realm, which is very dangerous when it comes to your soul. When Cain killed his brother Able, the lord said Abel's blood spoke out from the ground. The blood circulatory system is the soul of man, and without blood, the human body cannot live. The spirit of man is not affected in the process of dying because the spirit is eternal. I had a good friend who was given three days to live and beat the odds, and then one year later, he died. I thought if he had died one year before our meeting, I would have never had the pleasure of meeting him or gained such great insight from our friendship. There was also a young lady who was a dear friend of mine whom I met in the church's hallway, and she said with tears in her eyes I'm so tired of being sick, and she looked into my eyes with this sense of peace, and detachment from this physical realm. Then she told me she had been battling different illnesses for the last fourteen years of her life, and she was tired. She asked me not to tell anyone, so I agreed to pray for her, and two months later, she gave up the ghost. When I got word that she had passed away, I heard her voice within my spirit full of joy and laughter saying; Mac, it's so beautiful here, and all the people here are beautiful, and she went on rejoicing until that inner voice drifted away into silence. Warning! Demonic, wicked, and seductive spirits make deals with mankind, exchanging human souls. Many entertainers have made foolish deals with the devil and have turned so far from God in their imagination that it's impossible to turn back, which is the definition of someone selling their soul.

The Holy Spirit works just the opposite of everything evil, only imparting supernatural information into the spirit and heart of people seeking God. When we are moved by the Holy Spirit of God, we understand our original spiritual makeup.

Spiritual Dyslexia

The spiritual link in quantum physics unites every believer with Christ universally, forming the quantum dynamics of human behavior. Universally speaking, our cell structure does not differ from the universal solar system and the billions and billions of stars, planets, and galaxies. The first heaven is in the sky, where people often see images made of clouds. Alternatively, the second heaven, space, encompasses the first, allowing identification with celestial bodies such as stars and planets. The third heaven is the throne room of God, which is beyond space and time. Each part of the heavens has a three-part makeup, and then there is the outer dimension, which is identified as the seven heavens. Nitrogen, oxygen, and argon make up the first heaven. Celestial planets, dark energy, and zero gravity compose the second heaven. The third heaven is beyond every dimension known to man because it is 100% spiritually classified. Although we are physically present in this material world, the Holy Spirit has granted us access to the 7th heaven by using our imagination. The book of Revelation details the New Heaven, New Earth, and New Jerusalem existing beyond our current space and time. Human experience's most powerful element, the freedom of the mind, directs our daily lives by creating thoughts continuously. The Jewish nation, which was taught by Moses, shares this common idea of eternal bliss in the 7th heaven. Reading and understanding the word of God will renew your mind with supernatural insight from the Holy Spirit. Spiritual enlightenment will grant you power over the strongholds of the mind and give you authority to bind things and heaven and loose things on the earth. (Matthews 16:19).

People have conditioned many Christian believers to stroke the ego of man instead of depending on the spirit of God. There is a lack of spiritual growth in many congregational settings worldwide. People are perishing from the lack of knowledge. To conquer the ego, one must confess sins and repent daily. The culture of America has trained Americans from the day of birth with egotistical ideas of the flesh, selfishness, pride, and greed in the name of god. The key principle of American history was not founded on the Spirit of the word of God, but the content of the writings of the word of God, which have led many people to stray in their quest to truly understand God. Many organizations use the Bible for ceremonial only and totally reject the spirit of the bible for the power of conversion. We have developed a keen sense to reject the poor and dictate to the less fortunate rules and standards based on the color of our skin and social status.

Some have gone so far as to justify evil acts of the flesh as the will of God while enslaving men and women with physical acts of violence, mental and sexual abuse through the power of oppression. Jesus teaches his disciples a valuable lesson in Luke 11: 5-13 concerning the instruction of gaining power from the Holy Spirit. This power of the Holy Spirit can be granted through the persistence and determination of importunity. This means to never stop asking, seeking, and knocking on the doors of God for enlightenment as you walk the paths of Christ. When your walk with Christ becomes second nature, there will be times when you will slip, trip, and even be pushed down,

Spiritual Dyslexia

but you must get up and walk again. The scripture teaches that the spirit is willing to submit to the will of God, but the flesh is weak. (Matthews 26:41)

Paul speaks about having the will to do right but finding yourself doing wrong. This is a present sign that sin dwells within all believers, desiring to control us by sinful lust of the flesh. (Romans 7: 7-21) It is very important to gain a healthy understanding of confession and repentance of sin because it is the only remedy to control sin in our lives. If we hide our sins from God, it's just like Adam hiding from God in the Garden of Eden. The reason many people have a hard time understanding the bible is based on them not knowing the author of the bible. The Holy Spirit can be grieved in many ways when men and women do not realize His presence, and work in the world we live in. Then, some claim to possess special powers of healing and miracles for financial gain, which is not an uncommon practice amongst many members of the body of Christ. Paul testifies that these false doctrines would creep into the church unaware, and many will turn from the truth having itching ears to old wives' tales given in to seducing spirits of the flesh. In the book of Acts in the eighth chapter, a man who thought he could purchase the Holy Spirit with money faced Phillip. This man would be known in modern society as a drug dealer, palm reader, pimp, false prophet, or any other imposter sailing people with a false sense of hope for profit. Some of America's greatest drug dealers are set up on every corner in every neighborhood nationwide, known as pharmacies. Although there is a great need for medication today, we can't overlook the fact that it is all for profitable gain first, and not designed to help save lives.

The spirit that works behind greed, control, and evil influence is known as the anti-spirit. It opposes all that is good and perfect. Today, I read an article on social media that has given Satanists the right to introduce the most powerful satanic symbol the Baphomet into the public school system based on the Freedom of Religion Act. This satanic children's book teaches kids and adults how to summon up demonic forces for world gain and power, which has been displayed by some of the most powerful entertainers in the world today. This is not a coincidence, but an orchestrated plan of the spirit of darkness to destroy the gift of the human soul.

The antichrist is the arch enmity of every human, whether good or bad because he only comes to steal, kill, and destroy. Many people have read and understood the ancient story of the fall of Lucifer, the anointed angel that covered. In the book of Ezekiel, he is described as the exalted Worshiper Master over the Angelical host. Lucifer developed a rebellious spirit, which was the opposite of his intended purpose. His spirit of rebellion has dwelled on the planet Earth as the anti-spirit of God. The scripture testifies that if Satan had known what he was doing when he crucified Christ, he would have never crucified him. The scripture says the "kingdom of God suffers violence, and take it by force". Since all things have not taken their last place in time, presently Satan still takes advantage of any opportunity to ascend and descend from the throne room of God making accusations against the people of God with the false hope of getting God approvable to reject man. As the deceiver of the world, he works behind the scenes of the systems of the world with great technological advancements in science, and

Spiritual Dyslexia

human studies that reject the knowledge of God, creating a Godless civilization or second phase of human government. A lukewarm spirit person cannot see or understand the gross darkness that is set in the world all around them. They will go on trying to make logical sense out of the evil influence that is destroying the world. In the book of Ephesians, we are taught to pay attention to the times in which we live, because the day is evil. These acts of evil are being seen more today than at any other time in history.

For example, a 21-year-old man went into a church in Charleston, South Carolina, and killed 9 people as they attended bible study. Evil acts like this have occurred many times in the United States and will continue to occur because people lack education in Christ's prophecies about the beginning of sorrows. While these acts of terror grasp the attention of the world through media exposure, the unsuspecting Church ignores the fact that human beings are now being subject to micro-chipping to mark and control the population of the world by the old bait-and-switch method. Many Christians will not see clearly in these gross, dark times of evil influence in high places, because they have never seen the authority of God shown in their own lives. They have equated Christian living as acts of social and moral behavior of the flesh, which creates a false sense of confidence for a better world.

The story unfolds with five wise virgins and five unwise virgins that had lamps. These five wise virgins had lamps with oil in them, but the five unwise virgins had lamps with no oil in them. The parable of the ten virgins serves as a cautionary tale because many Christians awaiting Christ's return will face unmet expectations. Although there is very little teaching on the rapture in the Church today, it is an actual event that shall come to pass according to prophecy. This parable explains a time to come when many believers will become so lax in their faith that half of the believing body of God will become unprepared to meet Christ in his coming. Many commentaries view these scriptures as about Israel and her blindness, but we should not forget that God has no respective person. The scripture is very direct in its description that all ten characters of the parables were virgins, which meant they were all innocent and considered pure according to the flesh. Each virgin held a lamp while waiting for the bridegroom, strongly suggesting a time of darkness. Then, the parable divides the virgins into two groups, which are the wise and unwise. Christ teaches the congregation that the foolish virgin took their lamps but took no oil with them, and the wise took their lamp with oil in them. Then he tells them all ten virgins became tired and went to sleep. When the clock struck midnight, a cry went up, and the bridegroom arrived to meet his bride. All the virgins turned on their lamps, but the lamps of the foolish virgins did not light up because they did not have any oil. Then, the unwise turned to the wise virgins and begged them for their oil, but they refused to share their oil and told them they had to go buy their oil. In a panic, the unwise virgins went to get oil for themselves, but it was too late because Christ had come and gathered out the elect sake that had prepared to meet him, and when the unwise returned with oil, the Church was gone!

Colossians 1:13 fulfills the prophecy of Isaiah 60:2, showing how God's children must stand confidently in the Lord during times of great darkness. Until we teach the church truth according to the word of God, then there is no way that we will escape the grips of these forces of evil. Jesus Christ alone dispels darkness; only He provides that light. This prophecy was Isaiah's, written about 700 years before Christ. Paul wrote a letter to the Colossians about 70 years after the death of Christ, which teaches the believer how to have hope and understanding during a time of evil affliction. Behold, darkness will cover the earth, and gross darkness will engulf the people. Who has delivered us from the power of darkness and has translated into the kingdom of his dear Son? These two profound scriptures will empower the believer by the spirit of God to walk in divine light during darkness. The spirit of God speaks expressly to those who have an ear to hear. While many professing Christians become drawn away from the chaos of the world, the true believer should take this time to gather information and insight from the spirit realm on how to stand against the wiles and tricks of the devil. Amidst tragedies, many questions arise, yet things often remain unchanged, preventing proper change from occurring. The societies of the world have become so accustomed to doing the same thing, expecting a different result, which is defined as insanity. If you have not taken the time to receive Christ as your lord and savior, I admonish you to take this Holy Spirit invitation by saying, "Lord, I am a sinner, and I need saving from the coming wrath of God. Lord God, I confess that my heart is not right, and there are so many impure things that I have done to shame thee, as well as myself. Lord God, when I die, I do not want to go to hell and spend eternity separated from thee. Dear God, please have mercy on me, and receive me my soul as your own, and remove everything within me that is not like you, so that I may be free to serve thee, and reign with thee for all eternity. With this confession of faith, I give myself to thee with the full assurance that Christ die for me, and set me free from the grips of sin and death for all eternity; in Christ Jesus' Name, AMEN.

CHAPTER

2

THE FOOLISHNESS OF PREACHING

One of the first rites of passage to get divine insight begins with Paul's invocation of the Spirit of God and its presence within the believer of Christ. God enacted a plan of salvation, paradoxically, through preaching that some considered foolish. To the people who don't believe Christ is real, I want to say I truly understand. I wrote this chapter in reflection on a time in my life when I shared the same point of view. I believed Christ was not that important as long as I did good deeds in life. My belief system prioritized material wealth, yet I felt charitable acts, however small, would appease a higher power, should one exist. I opposed the church, believing—as many do today—that it was a money-making scam, a false reality, and foolish to be caught in such an illusion. My lack of faith didn't stop me from wondering about the universe's operation.

It would be many nights that I would stare into heaven and wonder what was keeping all things in place and what was the mind of the being that was controlling and creating it all. My childhood memories include unforgettable Sunday morning sermons heard at church with my mother. I viewed the Church as a punishment, not realizing I stood between the carnal and spiritual realms. I was living in the darkness and neglecting the very thing I needed by avoiding the truth. My fear, judgment, and expectation of damnation distorted my understanding of God's true nature and His love for mankind. By the foolishness of preaching, I learned personally that Christ is good for me regardless of whether anyone else agreed!

Preaching is the direct spoken word of God through his chosen vessel to communicate his will, love, and concerns for the families of the earth. The scriptures testify that God, through the foolishness of preaching, reveals his salvation plan for mankind; whoever calls on the name of Jesus will be saved. How then shall they call on him if they have not believed? Alternatively, how can they call on one they have not heard of? And how shall they hear of him without a preacher? And how can they preach unless they are sent? As it is written, how beautiful are the feet of them that preach the Gospel of peace, bring glad tidings of good things. (Romans 10:1-13)

God instituted the concept of preaching the word of God himself for our soul's salvation and should always demonstrate the purest form of his love, which will lead mankind into fellowship with his creator. This direct approach to communication should always offer peace to a worried soul while inspiring glad tidings to a restless spirit and restoring hope to

Spiritual Dyslexia

hopeless situations of the flesh. God's preached word aims to edify the believer's spirit, mind, and soul. It is the Preacher's great responsibility to tell the body of Christ about their ultimate hope in Jesus Christ. For over 2000 years, God's message has remained consistent: no one can be saved except through Jesus Christ. The long-awaited Messiah had finally come into the world to save his people from their sins by the preached words of John the Baptist at the Jordan River; "'Behold, the Lamb of God, who takes away the sin of the world!." John 1:29. This proclamation of salvation still rings free from the pulpits of every church of God all around the world today, as the Good News. Replacing the gospel of grace with a secular approach of legalism directly insults the magistrate of God's divine indwelling, polluting God's free gift. Humanity's moral and social practices transform the good news when we remove grace from God's plan of salvation. A preacher has a divine duty to present themselves to God as a living sacrifice in Christ. Being a living sacrifice requires daily surrendering of the flesh and repentance of known and unknown sins. By the confession of sin and submission to the word of God, we enter into his guiding light, which will direct you out of the darkness. The vessel of God must have a consecrated heart and conscience so the Holy Spirit may flow faithfully through you as a person of God. This does not mean that the chosen vessel of God is not sinful, but it means this person understands the sanctification process, so they shall not think themselves more highly than they ought to! Preachers, mindful of their own past failings, should shepherd their congregations with conscientious awareness. I beseech you therefore by the mercies of God that you present your bodies as a living sacrifice holy, and acceptable unto God which is your reasonable service, and be not conformed to this world: by the transforming of your mind that you may prove what is acceptable, and perfect will of God (Romans 12:1-2) The overall goal of preaching the word of God is to communicate effectively on all level what is the full council of God and his promises, power, and purpose for all.

Because of its spiritually based format designed to stimulate believers' minds, people worldwide commonly use expository preaching in their congregations. A preacher effectively communicates biblical doctrine, connecting spiritual concepts to enhance the congregation's understanding of the spiritual realm and God. This simply means that preaching is most effective when the preacher stays within the text of the scripture, extracting only what is written. When we read into things that are not written in the text, we can create a great deal of confusion for people who are potential Christ seekers. Many people believe the spirit of the prophetess Anna, the first woman missionary, originated the nuns, but this theory ignores the fact that she was a widow and had been married. There are no references to nuns in the Bible. Many forms of false doctrine will produce a form of godliness without the power of God. False doctrine will have many people learning but never able to come to the knowledge of truth, overlooking the fact that human ideology can never supersede the wisdom of God. Preaching is not telling people what you think they want to hear for self-gratification based on crowd participation. Paul tells his young portage Timothy to remain steadfast in the scripture as he charged him to preach the word, in season, and out of season: reprove, rebuke, exhort

Spiritual Dyslexia

with all long suffering in doctrine. He warns Timothy about an approaching time when people will not endure sound doctrine but, after their own lust, appoint teachers who will tickle their ears and deny the truth. 2nd Timothy 4:3 mentions that some individuals preach God's word for personal gain, like hirelings or wolves in sheep's clothing. God gives the preacher the ability to increase the faith in the lives of people. The Preacher of the word of God must act as a watchman on the wall, warning the flock of God of any preceding danger that may creep in unaware and cause swift destruction in the Church. (Ezekiel 33:1-7) The word of God came to me: Son of man, speak to your people, and say unto them: when I bring the sword against the land choice men and make them watchman, and when he sees the sword coming against the land, he shall blow his trumpet to warn the people. The people are responsible for their actions if they ignore the warning; however, the watchman is also responsible if they cannot give a warning. Son of man, I have made you a watchman for the people of Israel; I have also given this responsibility to the laity and preachers of God's church. Although Preaching is not based on a great multitude of fancy words, you must speak effectively with sound doctrine while delivering your sermon. For effective communication, sermon titles must clearly reflect the subject matter, providing listeners with a helpful context. We should always consult the aid and guidance of the Holy Spirit to connect to the spirit of the people for edification within the body of the Church. When praying in church, do not be like the hypocrites praying long, thinking you will persuade the people by the multitude of your words. (Matthew 6:5). Ministers should pray for their congregations as

Christ taught his disciples—with mercy for themselves, others, and even enemies, and with gratitude for daily blessings. When you feel compelled to pray to God, find a secluded place, as Jesus did when he left his disciples to pray. Preachers do not have the right to teach God's people with a spirit of avoidance, trying to be none non-confrontational, stepping all around the truth to spare the feelings of people who may be in error. You must be mindful that you have to give an account for the souls of the people that God has called you to watch over.

The Book of Jeremiah contains a strong warning against pastors who scatter God's flock. God appoints and anoints pastors after his own heart, which is one of the hidden mysteries of the Church. Homosexuality, fornication, and adultery are not issues. These major sins have stained the pages of world history for centuries, so preaching around the subject will not change the fact that this is a grievous sin that needs to be dealt with, just like many sins. An ex-homosexual can be called by God for the service to preach and teach the word of God, but a deviant homosexual has no right to lead anyone in the things of God. Now, technology has trained us to believe that carrying a bible is an inconvenience, which causes a greater disconnect from the word of God. Technology has its place as a tool for the intent of preaching and studying the word of God, but it should never replace the word of God. When preachers replace the word of God with technology, they preach by notation instead of revelation. Technology moves at a greater rate of speed that normally affects short-term memory only. A preacher must be mindful that God is using you to speak for him, and he will confirm what you are saying, so you have to stay in fellowship with

Spiritual Dyslexia

him. Preachers have been called from all kinds of lifestyles, so do not look at the outer parts of a person, but look within the heart of a person. Preachers should always remember and share their testimony, but it should not be so overbearing that it overshadows your responsibility for lifting Jesus to draw all man unto him. Testimonies are the most important point of a redeemed life of Christ, but the intended purpose is not to become boastful of things done in the flesh, neglecting the fact it took the spirit of God to redeem you, and it's going to take the same Spirit of God to keep you. You did not choose me, but I chose you and appointed you, so you might go and bear fruit that will last, and what you ask in my name, the Father will give to you. (John 15:16) Paul teaches the Corinthians that there is no way to say that Jesus is lord without the Holy Spirit revealing that to you, so keep your focus on Christ! Ignore those men who boast of supernatural God-given gifts but have only showcased them on stages and platforms to amass wealth for themselves. These false prophets never showed these miracles and healing in places such as hospitals, mental institutions, or prisons. We have a duty charged by Christ to feed the hungry, attend to the sick, visit the prisoners, and clothe the naked. Don't take your call lightly or as an opportunity to get rich by taking advantage of people, because big does not always mean better, and a great following does not mean a great anointing. God removed King Saul's anointing in his second year, despite his having reigned over Israel for over 40 years. God can remove your anointing while you still hold the position, and it is very costly to your spirit, mind, and soul. The anointing will reveal patterns in a person's life in a manner that most people would not even imagine. Christ is the container of the word of God, which activates the navigation system that directs preachers. The anointing is something much greater than patterns, styles, and words developed from the logic of the understanding of man. Truly, receiving the anointing after accepting Christ as Lord and Savior brings unparalleled freedom. This peace transcends all understanding and remains inexplicable. It's the power and core of all truth that will direct and guide you even during troublesome times. The anointing is the same for all believers, so we have the right and privilege to exercise it as we please by flowing in it. In the Old Testament, they would use oil to anoint the people of God, and the oil ran down their faces and bodies, demonstrating the purity of God. Although there are many variations of how the anointing flows from person to person according to biblical truth. Preaching God's word rests on the premise that God loved the world so much that he gave his only begotten son so that whoever believes in him will be saved.

The devil tempts God's children using three main strategies: lust of the eye, lust of the flesh, and pride of life. (1 John 2:16) The Preacher of God has the sole duty and purpose of ministering the word of God in season and out of season. He shepherds God's people, overseeing the flock and helping the sheep overcome the wicked ones because God entrusted them to him. The minute that a preacher sees the people as his people and not God's people, then he or she is operating by the lust of the flesh, which will lead to the removal of the anointing of God. When a preacher's eyes become enlightened by worldly material gain of deception, then he or she is also operating

Spiritual Dyslexia

outside of the anointing of God. Worldly lusts and desires cause preachers to act with pride, completely outside God's anointing, endangering both them and their congregations. Ensure the flock receives adequate food, water, and care. Overlooked or unattended sheep will stray. Therefore, this responsibility is great. For many years, a subjectivist mindset type of leadership, which stems from a spirit of control and greed, has led the urban church. This is a very dangerous spirit to adopt as the people of God because it is just another form of slavery. Subjective mind control, like a venomous poison, severely harms God's objectively thinking people. Subjectivism takes the freedom out of creativity, visions, love, and faith and places everything in practical reasoning, which creates dangerous yokes among the people of God. The flocks of God will comprise all kinds of lifestyles, experiences, and backgrounds, so there must be a non-biased approach to preaching the word of God. When we preach from a subjective mind state, we are no longer open to the objective flow in which God can freely communicate with us. When God's people are subject to your own personal values, culture, and religious ideas, the sheep will become subject to the theories of man. Without an objective, open mind, it is next to impossible to preach the word of God. Many traditional preachers considered the very thought of change: discard, strife, and envy (born of pride). Many years ago, while I was sitting in church listening to a very basic sermon being preached, I felt conflicted in my spirit, and something spoke to me in a very still voice, saying a preacher should never be subjective but objective when preaching or teaching the word of God.

The Israelites became so focused on God's law that they nullified it, replacing God's intended love with legalism. I often hear Christians celebrate their avoidance of interfaith interaction, viewing it as evidence of their outstanding faith. Once, I was teaching in a particular church and brought a Quran and Torah with me to use as an example of the cultures of Abraham's offspring. Surprisingly, they rejected my message despite the Quran and Torah being historical guides that shape church culture. Objective thinking is a pattern of thought that is unbiased and that personal prejudices do not influence likes or dislikes based on facts.

Objective-thinking preachers will cultivate the world with the unique ability to articulate the word of God with purpose, love, passion, meaning, grace, creativity, and freedom. The subjective preacher will remain in black and white with a message of doom and gloom for anyone who is not subject to their religious ideology. There are seven primary colors and seven letters found in a rainbow: red, orange, yellow, green, blue, indigo, and violet. You are free to paint the gospel of grace in any manner that the spirit leads you to do so without fearing that you are breaking some rule of thumb. Theological Apologetic: A very important tool for preaching in the church today. The ministerial style of preaching demonstrates the need for repentance with a sincere heart. In the bible, from Genesis to Revelation, God would always explain the offense he had with his people. This is a normal process that is very vital to the growth of any ministry. The Bible explains how to deal with offense in the Church, as well as with your fellow neighbor. When we teach the Apologetic theology and don't deal with the offense, the same offense will keep occurring. God showed apologetics theology himself in Genesis 6 when he said that it had repented to him that he made man and was going to destroy all of mankind off the face of the earth until God found his grace reflecting unto him in the eyes of Noah. (Genesis 6:5-8) God himself speaks out in scripture and explains what offended him with man. After addressing the offense, God introduced his plan of salvation, prompting repentance. Noah preached the message of repentance for 120 years before the flood came, and likewise, the preachers of the church have this same charge to keep preaching the gospel of grace until Christ returns.

CHAPTER

3

JOB

The Book of Job is one of the most compelling books of the scripture. Much like the book of Revelation, many people danced around its historical content based on the lack of understanding. The question often arises: how could God allow a righteous, obedient man to suffer affliction at the hand of the devil as an act of love? Some scholars have referred to the book of Job as the metaphorical writings of Moses, and other scholars view Job as one of the oldest books of the bible in world history.

In this chapter, I will not debate between these two ideas concerning the life of Job, but will attempt to unlock the true hidden message of the book of Job, and the great conflict concerning his life and suffering!

Church history contains many commonly held beliefs regarding the life of Job, a righteous man who was, it seemed, a subject of conflict between God and the Devil. A man God classified as righteous and refused evil. The Bible tells an ancient story of Job being handed over to the devil and suffering great deals of affliction, which many people view as very abnormal, and conclude, according to Satan's report, that God rewards the righteous with injustice, concluding God must be impossible to please! This common view of God is a terrible illustration that has caused many people to err in the faith by logical reasoning. During the time of Common Era 3-4, when Jesus lived, in Matthew 7:21-23, Christ testifies about a group of people that were rejected by God, even after performing good works in God's name. Depart from me, you workers of iniquity! Satan has led many people to agree with the false idea that the bible contradicts itself! If even righteous workers couldn't escape God's wrath, who could?

The Bible tells us that Job, a resident of Uz, lived during the Edomite era, a time steeped in spiritual and magical allure. According to the Ancient writings of the book of Job, God reveals his authority over the spirit realm and the entire universe. Job 1:6. The book of Job describes mystic unicorn horses and large sea creatures. Mankind probably practiced sorcery, witchcraft, and black magic as a normal means of daily life. Scripture describes Job as blameless, upright, God-fearing, and averse to evil. He had seven sons and three daughters. His livestock comprised seven thousand sheep, three thousand camels, five hundred yoke of oxen, five hundred her asses, and a very great household. Studies suggest Job's life preceded Abraham's, portraying him as a significant, upright judge and community leader. Historians commonly share the view that Job's trials illustrate God's testing of humanity, a concept also reflected in the stories of Adam and Eve and the two trees in the Garden. As a believer, I understand trials are part of following Christ, but these narratives aren't about material tests; they're divine warnings. In both stories, we can see that suffering and grief accompanied these men's lives at the hands of Satan. The first question that I'm often asked concerning faith is why God would create a man and allow him to go through trials and suffering if he knew it would cause him to fall into sin. The most common answer is testing, which still leads to more open-ended questions. When taught that suffering is God's test, people see suffering as a terrible injustice from God. This thought process is so far from the truth. By close examination of the life and suffering of Job, I hope we all come to realize walking with God and performing acts of God are not the same! See, life must be about convictions and not preferences.

The first chapter of the Book of Job presents many conflicting issues surrounding Job's life. Many scholars conclude that Job's story depicts a test of faith between good and evil, focusing on material possessions. The second theory posits, inexplicably, that God needed to prove a point to Satan. When we look at the life of Job from that point of view, we foolishly believe Satan can tempt God. The scripture says that God does not tempt anyone with evil, and no man can tempt God with evil, so for many years, human logic and reasoning have caused us to make errors in our understanding concerning God and his motivates. When people of the faith are subject to trials, we should always ponder the thought of what's going on behind the scenes and how God gets glory out of the story. With the help of the Holy Spirit, God will unveil himself concerning the hidden mysteries of the scriptures. (Job 1:6) Now there was a day when the sons of God came to present themselves before the Lord Christ, and Satan came also amongst them, and the Lord confronts Satan, and asked him where has he been? Satan replies by saying he has been walking back and forth through the earth, going up and down in it. Then the Lord asks Satan a question concerning his servant Job, and Satan replies by saying you have a hedge around him, and you have blessed the works of his hands and caused him to prosper, but if you remove the hedge of protection, I will cause him to curse you to your face, so the Lord permitted Satan to touch all of Job's family members and material possession, but Satan could not touch him physically.

Job's affliction starts in his mind!

Being a devout man who valued sacrifice, Job offered additional sacrifices for his sons, ensuring God's favor. Although Job had a sincere concern for the hearts of his sons, he did not recognize the needs of his own heart. Like Job, we sometimes believe more sacrifice means more favor with the Lord. According to the scripture, Job was a righteous man, and his sacrifice was not in vain, but they seemed based on ritual and routine. Many Christians today share Job's moralist approach to God! Many believers truly believe they can use the Lord just to get what they want. This moralist ideology creates a false sense of hope, causing many people to err in the faith. This moralist approach is one of the root causes of the division among the Churches of Christ. Like Job, many people today attempt to appease God with good works, mistakenly believing that spiritual rewards will follow. God expects good fruit to come out of

Spiritual Dyslexia

the lives of every believer, but the approach must be in the right order. The old saying goes, you can't put the buggy in front of the horse, and you can't put good works before your faith. Your faith should produce good work, but good works can't produce faith! Many people will do good work, even though they don't believe in God. The anti-Christ will do many wonderful works of healing and miracles, even fooling some of the elect's sake of God. Jesus spoke the spirit of moralist behavior in a parable as he explained a story about two men going to the temple to pray. (Luke 18)

Job's moralist righteous behavior even had Satan fooled. Satan is not God, so he cannot see within the heart of man, but God searches the hearts of man and angels. Satan had nothing to accuse Job of. At Satan's request,... Although Job suffered the great losses of family and wealth, he remained steadfast concerning his moralistic ideas about the Lord, so he never physically sinned or charged God foolishly. His mindset seemed to be focused on the idea that he already had it bad, so he needed to make things even worse by questioning the Lord. Job says things he thought he should say, even though it was not from his heart. Just saying what we think God wants to hear is not the same as having a confessing heart. The Holy Spirit, through God's word, must break and mend our hearts wounded by sin.

Job's remarkable human resolve proved insufficient against the forces at play in his life. Satan returned to the throne of the Lord to accuse the brethren, but he still didn't have any accusations against Job in his reports. The Lord asked him a second time about his servant Job, and Satan responded by saying: Job may not have cursed you to your face behind losing his family and material things, but if you allow me to touch his health, then he would surely curse you to your face, so it was granted to Satan to afflict Job in the flesh, but he could not touch his soul. Then Job faced sickness and boils that grew all over his body, and again Job did what he knew to be right and sat down in sackcloth and ashes as a physical symbol of debasement and mourning to get the Lord's attention, which is a real demonstration of a broken heart seeking repentance from the Lord, and yet Job still did not cry out his true feelings to his creator. The hardest time for believers to truly trust God is during times of affliction. Job's wife said unto him, do you still keep your integrity? Curse God and die, but Job said to his wife you sound like a foolish woman. Should I receive well from the hand of God and shall not receive evil? In this, Job did not sin with his lips. Job spoke with confidence and never blamed God, but when it came to his physical health, he seemed to only be speaking from his lips and not his heart. The Church has become big on avoiding key issues within the body of the church, but still speaks out as if the Church is truly being blessed. People have fallen away from the Church in great numbers, and the church is sitting down in sackcloth and ashes. Job's three friends came to visit him with the same moralist reasoning based on the culture and religious routines. They act out their religious beliefs with Job for seven days and seven nights, trying to help him understand how he must have done something morally wrong to bring this curse upon him and his family. Job speaks and curses his date of birth to get God's attention by rebuking his own life with a cry of death. One of his friends showed a sense of compassion and soft rebuke by telling Job he got out of line

Spiritual Dyslexia

with God somewhere. His idea was God doesn't allow this type of calamity to fall on a person who is doing the right things, ensuring Job was reaping something he had sowed. Job justifies his actions and asks his friend to pity him because he has done nothing wrong. The friends only added more grief and sorrow to the information they shared with him, while Job felt like he was on the brink of death. For example, visiting an incarcerated person and reminding them of their mistakes won't help. Job turns his lamentation towards God, and for the first time, Job is directing attention towards God, but he still tries to make atonement by will power of the flesh by saying all the right things, neglecting the fact that sin is a heart issue. Job talks about God but never talks to God! The second friend confronts Job by telling him to stop acting and own up to what you have done. Job's friend was saying Job's entire plea bargaining was a waste of time. A moralist believer will always look at suffering as the result of disobeying God. In the gospels, when Jesus healed a blind man, his disciples asked him who had sinned, his father or mother. Jesus said neither one has sinned. Job speaks of the justice of God, understanding that no one can question God's truth, knowing God has hundreds of questions that man can never understand. For many years, the Church has taught this doctrine of moralistic, ritualistic religion. The scriptures clearly say to repent daily, and even if a man falls seven times, God will lift him up. This false doctrine has kept a great multitude of people out of the church because the reality is no one has lived up to this standard.

Job's friends were blind guides to the truth of God's will! Then Job's other friend rebukes Job, saying this makes little sense. There is no way that God would have allowed this to happen to you if you had done right, so obviously, you are lying. Job responds by saying I understand how God works, and I gave all the right sacrifices, and yet I'm afflicted, but his friends persisted Job had sinned before God. The only response the Lord recognizes is praise and worship. Like Job, the Church has come up with many formulas that are supposed to grant you favor with the Lord. Job had to realize that his formula for God was not working! It wasn't until 41 chapters later that Job finally came to himself after being confronted by God for his vain attempts to make God his puppet and servant. The life of Job is like the beauty of a rose in full bloom, while attached to a stem full of thorns. It is possible to become very idle while working within the church if the heart isn't right with God. That God's love has set us free and fulfills us. God is the sacrifice that he requires of himself, to himself, by his self, for his self. Receiving him for who he is, not for what he gives, truly sets us free.

Now, let's look at the life of Enoch compared to the life of Job. In the book of Genesis 5: 21, we find the seventh man born from Adam named Enoch. Enoch lived 65 years and bore a son, Methuselah, the oldest man in history, who died in 969. He was one of the few seven men in scripture to live over nine hundred years. According to the Torah, he died seven days before Noah entered the ark, escaping the great flood. These were Godly men of the lineage of Seth, who thought men to call upon the name of the lord after his older brother Cain killed their other brother Abel. Enoch walked with God, and God took him, which is an example of the rapture of all those who are absent from the body present with the lord. Scholars found his life's testament among the Dead Sea Scrolls. The author of the Book of Enoch wrote it much like the Book of Revelation, presenting angel beings and figurative, symbolic, and literal messages. The seven mountains in Enoch 25 correspond to the seven candlesticks described in Revelation 1. Enoch prophesied that the blessed elect and righteous will survive the tribulation and then eradicate wickedness. And he took up his parable and said, Enoch, a righteous man, who God opened his eyes, saw visions of the Holy One in the heavens. The angel showed me, and I heard everything, and from them, I understood everything as I saw, but not for this generation, but a remote one which is to come concerning the elects. I said and took up my parable concerning the holy Great one who will come forth out of Mount Sinai and appeared in the strength of his might from the heavens Enoch 1: 1-4. This vision and parable is the first and oldest prophecy of the Rapture Church before the tribulation period begins, which is confirmed by the brother of Jesus in the 14 verses of the book of Jude. When we look at the righteousness of Job and the righteousness of Enoch, we can see a great contrast in the difference between Enoch walking with God and Job sacrificing to God. Enoch's great-great-grandson, Noah, lived in a very wicked time and understood the importance of having a relationship with God not a religion in God.

    During that time, fallen angels influenced men and women, causing them to defile themselves with charms, enchantment, and cutting of roots and plants for intoxication. The Godly seed of Seth had become tainted with sin for marrying the ungodly daughters of Cain and then impregnating them. The fallen angel cast spells on the people and put porn graphics thoughts in the hearts and minds of mankind, producing a wicked outcome. It repented the Lord that he had made man upon the face of the earth, and it grieved him at his heart, and the lord said, I will destroy man whom I created from the face of the earth, both man and beast and all living things, but Noah found Grace in the eyes of the Lord. Noah, a just and perfect man in his generation, walked with God. Therefore, the Lord sent the angel Uriel, a master craftsman skilled in building measurements, to Noah, giving him plans and resources to build the Ark of the Covenant. This was the only provision given by God to escape the final judgment of the planet Earth for the unconfessed sins of humanity. Some also view the ark as a type of Christ. As a place of protection, the Ark provided a shield of faith while the rest of the world faced destruction. Christ testifies, saying that the signs of my second coming will be like the days of Noah, and again, we can see that there is a strong contrast of difference when it comes to Noah's relationship with God and Job's religion about God. (Matthew 24:37). Abraham was the son of Terah, who was very successful in his occupation of making images out of wood and stone as representations of god. People would buy these images and pray over them to meet their various needs, but Abraham's heart was not content with this form of idol worshipping, which often led him to wonder about the creator of the heavens and the earth. The Lord told Abram to leave his family and go to a land He would reveal, promising to make him a great nation, to make his name great, and to bless those who blessed him and curse those who cursed him. Genesis 12: 1-3. Abraham gathered his family and made his first steps of faith as God imputed righteousness in him; he trusted God without seeing the results of his appointed destination, so again, we can see plainly that there is a significant contrast difference in Abraham's faith in God and Jobs practices in God. The Bible is our manual that reveals the mind of God concerning his love and plans for humanity. God gave Abraham the promise in the fourth dispensation of time, attesting to how God credits righteousness to a believer's spirit. Abraham walked with God, and by open demonstration, he will sacrifice his son Isaac, the promised seed. With the eyes of faith, he saw and understood the parable of Christ that reads, except the fruit falls from the tree and dies, it can't reproduce other fruit. Abraham became the known father of all three Holy books of Spiritual dialectic. The believers of Christ have been indulging with the power of the Holy Spirit to release spiritual insight into humanity with a message of love, confrontation, and peace during perilous times. Ishmael's spirit appeared in the life and practices of the great prophet Mohammed, who was God's last human lawgiver and messenger, as the son of Abraham. Mohammed taught that those who reject God and hinder man from the path of God will die rejecting God, and there shall be no forgiveness, which is in line with the teaching of Moses and Christ. The three teachings of Abraham—the Holy Bible, the Holy Quran, and the Holy Torah—reveal the beauty and wonders of understanding God's design for humanity.

The author did not write this chapter about Job to dismiss his righteousness, but used comparisons with other righteous men in scripture to help the reader understand that human acts of righteousness will never please God. In the 32nd chapter through the 37th chapter of the book of Job, the prophet Elihu is angry with Job and his three friends because they did not understand Job's suffering. The very answer they sought was never obtained. Elihu confronts the men for their logical reasoning idea of God being unjust in the affairs of man. He reminds them that God formed man from clay, and therefore, we cannot be justified by any acts of the flesh. The young prophet says Elihu spoke again, saying, you think your righteousness is greater than God? Indoctrination teaches us to trust God through human efforts based on human logic, which cancels out faith altogether. Throughout the 38th and 40th chapters, we see Job humbling himself after being confronted by God concerning his vain religious obligations. The book of Job concludes with Job repenting to God and God restoring him with double for all that he lost. The book of Job should stand as a constant reminder that God can truly receive only a broken, contrite heart that trusts in Christ. I hope Christ's divine relationship helped you in your quest to become one with your creator.

CHAPTER

4

HERITAGE

For centuries, the history of the bible has been told through the eyes of many people! So often, others overlook the original people in depictions of their own lives and history. Their legacy becomes hidden in the unawareness of plain view. This hidden history of the world was influenced by evil forces working behind the scenes to destroy the rich history of the Melanated People, who have served and worshiped the creator of heaven and earth with great passion. Powers of darkness and its chief engineer, Satan, who foreknew without a doubt that he could destroy humanity by stripping us of the rich heritage of worshipping and severing our God, led this evil agenda. His plan of temptation started with the first man, who was a melanated individual. God created him from the dust of the ground and created a woman from his rib. In the writing of this book, I would like to revisit the history of people, places, and ideas that books, movies, and pictures have distorted. A personal point of view in history writing empowers and controls the narrative from the author's perspective. This Treasure Box of Biblical Heritage will enlighten your spirit with eye-opening facts concerning the power and influence of melanated people and their heritage in the Holy Bible. Our hearts and minds have been blind concerning the descendants of Adam, causing us to forfeit our rich inheritance given by the great God IAM that I Am. There were seven key Black men in Adam and Eve's time. Each of them lived for over 900 years. These seven men were Adam 932, Seth 912, Enos 950, Caiman 910, Jarred 962, Methuselah 969, and Noah 950. These seven men were the original descendants of Adam, and each one of them had a special call on their lives to affect the history and future of mankind. God's nature, as the Eternal Father, is entirely separate from the racial sins of Cain, which stem from humanity's flawed ego and its delusions of grandeur. Satan was the mastermind behind this evil influence of the egotistic beastly world system that operates out of greed, fear, and control. He offered Christ the throne of all the material kingdoms and governments of the world if he would feed his ego and worship him. Christ rebuked him with the power of his words, so he had to flee. The devil tried to use the same strategy that he used on Eve and Cain, but it did not work with Christ. John 1:14 states that God's word became flesh, fulfilling the prophecy in Isaiah 53:1-12 and 54:13-17. We should impart this teaching to all of Adam's descendants to counteract Satan's ongoing attacks, ensuring that no weapon formed against them will succeed. When Jesus said to turn the other cheek, he was basically saying to defuse

Spiritual Dyslexia

all threatening situations by the power of the Holy Spirit. The power of Jim Crow laws were the enter workings of Satan to kill, steal, and destroy the rich heritage of a God-fearing people. There is no way to justify the insensitive evil acts that destroyed Tulsa, Oklahoma, in 1921 and the countless acts of race riots in America. Those communities of melanated people were very successful and wealthy Black communities. Tulsa could overcome all the hate and violence that shaped America while creating Black Wall Street.

The Maccabees were a dark complexion Hebrew family who were the leaders of the Hebrew rebellious army that took control of Judea. The authority of the Seleucid Empire 312bc-63bc, which was written between the Old and New Testament writings, had conquered them. When the armies of Greece had taken power and control over the world, evil became a stronghold over the people of the planet. Israel had wicked men who created a covenant with the heathen nations and defiled the temple, which caused the downfall of Israel. The Greek men gained a reputation for doing great evil deeds, so they willingly submitted to the wicked roots of Seleucid idols in Jerusalem, and they offered sacrifice to the Greek gods after the likeness of heathen nations. Israel had rebelled against God, and the prophecies of Isaiah, Jeremiah, and Daniel were coming to pass. Israel forsook the covenant of God and failed to circumcise the male children on the eighth day as an open sign of rebellion against God. God was not pleased and gave them over to their enemy as he said he would, and Israel had become subject to her capturers. The Menorah was no longer burning in the temple of Jerusalem, and God had left Israel. King Ptolemy of Egypt had also succumbed to the power of this evil regime that had taken the world by force under the leadership of Alexander and his great navy. Matthias Maccabees and his five sons had a purpose in their hearts and minds to stand against the evil working of Greece with great expectation that God would give them victory. While Matthias sat in the temple, he saw the commissioner of Greece make a sacrifice offering to the idol Greek gods, so he killed him. News of Matthias' defiance reached the king, who dispatched a thousand men, Matthias and his forces slew them all. This enraged the king, and he pursued Matthias and his sons, but each time Matthias slaughtered his armies. He remembered how God delivered Goliath into the hands of David, and he stood firm on the promises of Abraham.

―――――― ✦✦✦✦✦✦ ――――――

During the 1800s, brothers and real estate brokers John and Augustus Allen bought 6,600 acres of swamp land in the southern United States for five thousand dollars. Other Realtors of that time thought the two brothers had lost their minds to spend so much money on such a gloomy and unproductive place. Back then, people viewed melanated men as unlearned, ignorant, or unintelligent. The Allen brothers seemed to fulfill the stereotypes shared amongst the Anglo-Saxon community until the brothers named their property after Sam Houston, who had won the battle of San Jacinto and became the president of the Government of Texas. The murky swamp land had become one of the greatest ports in the United States, and the city of Houston is now the 4th largest city in America and one of the energy and industrial capitals of the world. Today, Allen Parkway stands as a memorial to the two melanated brothers who did not allow the thoughts of others to limit them from reaching their full potential. Their vision paved the way and opportunity for one of America's greatest African American communities, known as Freeman's Town, with great community leaders such as the father and son duet, Jack and Rutherford Yates. John Henry Jack Yates was an American slave born on July 11, 1828, in Gloucester, Virginia. He moved to Houston in 1865 and purchased land in Free Man's Town 4th ward. He became the first melanated pastor of Antioch Missionary Baptist Church in Downtown Houston in 1868. Jack Yates later founded Bethel Missionary Baptist Church in Free Man's Town in 1891 on the corner of the red brick road. Andrew and Crosby, after the board of Antioch, refused to allow him to expand the Church. Yates established the Houston Academy for African Americans, and legends say Bethel Baptist Church was a safe house for slaves traveling with Harriet Tubman and the Underground Railroad. Rutherford Yates was an educator and owned a printing press company. His home is now a museum in Free Man's Town on Andrew St., a couple of blocks from his father's church. My great-grandmother, who was born in the late 1800s, stayed in the 4th Ward on Crosby St., right behind Bethel Baptist Church. The church baptized my mother, aunts, uncles, and cousins, and they attended there. One hundred-two years later, in 1989, Pastor Robert O. Robertson, the pastor of the last congregation to worship at Bethel Baptist Church of Freeman's Town before the arson, ordained me as a minister of the gospel. They have turned the church into a beautiful museum. Their skin color and status as freed slaves did not deter these men of faith from fulfilling their destiny.

In 1936, Jesse Owens' four gold medals shocked the world, discrediting Adolf Hitler's ideology of Aryan supremacy. The world watched as the Berlin Games was overtaken by a melanated man who displayed the greatest performance in the history of the Olympiad. Owens won the gold medal in the 100-meter dash, long jump, 200-meter, and 4x100-meter relay. The sad reality is the President of the United States did not even congratulate Jesse Owens for the victory America had gained over the Nazi dictator. His spirit to succeed helped pave the way for so many other melanated people, such as Venus and Serena, who have demonstrated triumph and victory as world Olympiads, as well as Carl Lewis, one of the few Olympians to gain four gold medals in a single World Olympics after the likeness of Jesse Owens.

Achieving freedom remains a gradual process for Black Americans, whether they are descendants of immigrants or born in the U.S. Every step of the way has been a conscious effort to overcome the barrier of racial tension, hate, and violence with intentional force to hurt, damage, and kill melanated people. When God breathed life into Adam's nostrils, the dust of the earth became a living soul created to worship his creator. God sees the mindless attacks on Black people, and those who intend to kill, steal, and destroy will face eternal damnation with Satan. The Civil Rights Movement of the United States of America was a demonstration of power under control as men

Spiritual Dyslexia

and women of the South came together with a nonviolence protest against evil in high places. The teachings of Christ, especially the principle of "turning the other cheek," empowered the movement. His leadership of the Washington, D.C. freedom march culminated in his world-renowned "I Have a Dream" address, provoking outrage and animosity from people like J. J. Edgar Hoover, who established and ran the F.B.I. Although the hearts and minds of evil men like J. Edgar Hoover and Jim Crow plotted against melanated people, their marches, dreams, and legacy continue to move forward as God's guiding light directs our path through every dark situation. What we can learn most of all from these great people of the faith is their ability to see victory in the eyes of defeat. Human reasoning or circumstance shapes human willpower, but faith is the ability to trust in God freely, no matter what human reasoning or circumstance shows. The human willpower is very limited, but faith in God is unlimited. God granted every human being free will, but never granted the will to become independent from the creator, as happened with Lucifer and the fallen angels.

The lives of Adam and Eve have taught one of the greatest stories known to humanity, and that is the fact human willpower is not enough to keep you from falling to the lust of the flesh. Nelson Mandela's faith in God's plan empowered him to overcome 27 years of wrongful imprisonment and emerge victorious in his fight against injustice, proving that even the greatest leaders face defeat. His faith empowered his will by trusting in God, which granted him the victory seat of becoming the first Melanated People president of South Africa. Nelson Mandela's life is a very real depiction of the story of Joseph and

Egypt embodied in a different space and time. Often, when we read the bible, we focus on the Hebrew nation because of the promise of Father Abraham. We must not forget that there was no such thing as a Jewish nation until hundreds of years after Adam. The 4th dispensation saw God choose a nation for himself. Melanated People Men have always played very significant roles in world history since the beginning of time and have made some of the greatest impacts in society, but for some strange reason, the devil tried to erase their work and legacy. As Christ journeyed up Skull Mountain, our lord and savior had become overwhelmed and tired from the beating and torture by Roman soldiers as he carried his cross of crucifixion. Jesus preached, whosoever will come after me, let him take up his cross and follow me, which was a non-racial invitation to discipleship. As Christ was dying, a young Black man from Cyrene, North Africa, was among those chosen to carry the cross. Black men and women equally helped to shape biblical history, displaying steadfast faith and risking their lives for their mission work.

Jericho's prostitute, Rahab, trusted the God of Israel's power, sheltered Israelite spies, and, as a result, her family survived Jericho's conquest by Joshua. Rahab had the opportunity to become a hero in her city but stood firm in the faith, which has ranked her name among the heroes of the faith. It's a shared belief that behind every good man, there is an exceptional woman, such as Israel's greatest leader, Moses, and his wife, Zipporah, of Ethiopian descent. Then there is the melanated woman, Ruth, whose unsurpassed loyalty and devotion to her mother-in-law led to her becoming the wife and queen of King Boaz. Of course, all the Melanated women in the bible did not play a subservient role to a man, but many Melanated women stood in their power like the great Queen Sheba of South Africa, whose kingdom was one of the greatest kingdoms ever ruled by a woman. Her power, authority, and captivated King Solomon, the wealthiest and greatest Hebrew king, ultimately fell in love with her, leading to a private engagement. Legends say she conceived a son from him. Their union fused the Hebrew Law of God into the hearts and minds of the kingdoms of South Africa. The converted Hebrew people would follow the laws and the God of Israel. Queen Candace held the tradition of the South African traditions and religion, so she would send her Eunuch to Jerusalem with her treasures to give a yearly offering. Philip encountered her Black male servant, who became the first gentile South African convert to Christianity and then returned to Ethiopia to share the Gospel. The Bible has many references to the heritage, pride, and power of the people of the second-largest continent, Africa. Genesis 2:10-14 suggests the Garden of Eden was in eastern Africa, possibly in Ethiopia, according to the Bible. These four rivers flowed in the Garden of Eden: Pishon, Gihon, Tigris, and the Euphrates, which is referred to as the land of Cush, which means Ethiopia. Africa's enduring power and influence, from its diamond mines to prominent figures like Barack Obama Sr., continue to shape the modern world. A special program selected Obama to attend college in the United States at the University of Hawaii. The Obama couple gave birth to their firstborn child, Barack Obama the II, who became the first melanated President of the United States of America. President

Barack Obama II has been the most disrespected president in the history of America, with an open display of racial remarks. While the hateful spirit of some Americans attempted to destroy President Barack Obama's spirit and dreams, they ignored that both of his parents had economic educations, which helped reverse America's economic decline and financial crisis caused by the Bush administration. The 44th President of the United States of America, Barack Obama II, has created more economic surplus while granting health care coverage for all Americans. Michelle Obama, the first Black First Lady of the United States, is a lawyer and writer who gracefully supported her husband and raised their two daughters, Malia and Natasha, the first Black children raised in the White House. Decades before Barak Obama ever thought of obtaining the highest position in America, as the President of the United States lived a melanated woman by the name of Shirley Chisholm. In 1968, Shirley Chisholm was the first black congressional representative representing New York State in the House of Representatives for seven terms. She was the first African American to seek the presidency, achieving this in her 1972 Democratic nomination.

The American Creed

I believe in the United States of America as a government of the people, by the people, whose just powers the governed consent to, a democracy in sovereign states forming a perfect union established on the principles of freedom, equality, justice, and humanity for which American patriots sacrificed

Spiritual Dyslexia

their lives and fortunes. My love for my country compels me to uphold its constitution, laws, and flag, defending it against all enemies: America, the land of the free and the home of the brave, a freedom secured through sacrifice, particularly by people of color.

CHAPTER

BORN AGAIN

"But seek ye first the Kingdom of God, and his righteousness, and all these things shall be added unto you."—Matthew 6:33

The Bible's widespread impact notwithstanding, a growing estrangement between God and his creation is evident. This alarming fact is largely because of the reality the creation has worshiped the creation over the creator and turns a deaf ear to the voice of the Creator. Jesus: I am the good shepherd and know my sheep, and my sheep know me. As the father knows me, even so, I know the father, and I lay down my life for the sheep. I also have other sheep that is not of this fold, which I will bring also, and they shall hear my voice, creating one fold and one shepherd! (John 10: 14-16)

In this chapter you will learn the valuable lesson of distinguish the difference between the true voice of God, and the lies of Satan. God gives us clear clairvoyance concerning future events beyond your normal sensory known as prophecy. In the book of John we will gather information to help us understand the importance of being born again reconnecting to our spiritual being of divine source. Throughout history mankind has look through the physical eyes of humanity trying to understand the invisible eternal spirit of God. Nicodemus was a Pharisee, and a Jewish teacher of the Sanhedrin counsel. Sanhedrin counsel was assembly of 23-71 men appointed in every city in the Land of Israel.

> *They were a Jewish Supreme Court system of Religious men that lived during the time of the temple. The information that follows is the Munich Tamud manuscript of b. Sanhedrin 43a. According to the trial of Jesus of Nazareth's 43a, recorded in world history: as the controversial trail of Yeshu Notzen tells the story of Jesus the Christ. Nicodemus attended this trial, and even tried to peruse the counsel not to crucify Yeshus, but Satan plans to kill Christ was fully manifested, while the fulfilment of God plan of redemption was being demonstrated before the Heavens, and Earth. The censored ship begins its circulation around the 13 century from the original written manual script. The talk of the time was documented in the 43a written concerning Yeshu the Notzarina on the eve of Passover. An acritical begin to circulate saying: in 40 days*

Yeshu will be stoned for sorcery, and misleading and enticing Israel. A note was added to article saying anyone who knows anything in his defense must come forth, but no one came in his defense, and a warrant was issued for Jesus arrest. This acritical was recorded by Ulla bar Ishmael about ce. 70. When carting the times from Common era 300 to common era 001 it shows Christ was born about 3 c.e., and died 30 years later at the age 33. This information is base of the death of King Herod who died in c.e. 4. The recorded history of Yeshu has been dated, and signs in the acritical of the Sanhedrin counsel. His resurrection has been debated concerning the three day ordeal in the grave, and his resurrection one early Sunday morning. Many scholars have auger the point that if he was kill on Friday then Sunday would not have been third days as scriptures testify. Then there are historians' researchers that say a person death date should not change from March, and other years April. I found that Jesus instituted the observance of the Passover on the night of Nisan 14 according to the Jewish calendrer, and records show that Nisan 14, was a Wednesday April 1st 33 c.e. This is the day when there are exactly 12 hours of daylight, and 12 hours of darkness.

The first observation of the new moon nearest to spring equinox mark the first day of Nisan, and Passover began 13 days later which has unlocked the hidden mystery of the spiritual and physical Passover, which is the reason why Resurrection Sunday or Passover will change dates, and months. My personal understanding in the matter is that the Last supper took place on Wednesday Nisan 14, which lead to his arrest in the false trial that went on until the early hours of Thursdays morning and ended with his beating, and crucifixion Thursday afternoon, which led to Christ giving up the Ghost by Thursday evening. My personal calculation is that he was dead Thursday, Friday, Saturday, and resurrected early Sunday morning as Mary sought for him at dawn, which is about 6am when the Angel told her, he has risen like he said he would.

    A single divine source reveals the moral codes underlying all human communication, ancient texts, and diverse cultures; however, various interpretations produce similar but distinct understandings. Nicodemus, for example, witnessed Christ's miracles and acknowledged his divine nature, yet struggled to reconcile Christ's divinity, much like many believers today. Jesus told him that unless a man be born again, he could not see the kingdom of God, which led Nicodemus to ask an opposing question of how a man could be born a second time. Can a man reenter into his mother's womb? Jesus' answer was very conflicting because his response defied all human logic. Our inability to fully understand how the invisible became visible keeps many Christian believers, religious people, and unbelievers today from connecting with Christ's true identity. Colossians 1:15 Christ is the visible image of the invisible God and the firstborn of all creation. The Bible refers to him as the light of the world, and there is no material or physical image in pure light. Christ came forth as the first eternal being from the essence of eternal light and divine energy, which has no beginning or end, then he stepped into time from eternity as the Alpha and Omega, the physical eternal conscience, God. He was in the world, and the world existed by his hand, and the world knew him not. He came to his own, and they received him not. But many as received him, to them, he gave them power to become the sons and daughters of God. John 1: 10-12.

To hear the call of God, you must be born of the spirit of God. The Bible says that God is spirit, and those who worship him must worship him in spirit and truth. Nicodemus was a very religious man, but all of his religious understanding could not help him understand the Kingdom's message of Christ. In the 21st century, a significant spiritual disconnect within the church has prevented men and women of God from fully using their spiritual gifts to manifest God's kingdom on earth. God created Adam and Eve to create his will on earth as it is in heaven. Through the power of thought, we manifest spiritual things into the physical realm. The eternal spirit of God teaches each believer that there is an eternal sense of well-being to all that will receive Christ. This sense of well-being is the reconnection of man back to his divine source. Simply put, being born again means living from the spiritual to the physical and not living physical to the spiritual. Genesis 1:27

shows that God made man and woman in his spiritual likeness, and then in Genesis 2:7, in his physical likeness. This is the same illustration that Christ is using when he tells Nicodemus he that is born of Spirit is Spirit, and he that is born of the flesh is flesh. His lack of understanding compromised his faith, leading him to possess God's kingdom through logic. This led others to believe that works of the flesh bring salvation, even though scripture testifies that nothing good dwells in the flesh. (Romans 7:18) Martin Luther (1483-1546) was the founder of the Protestant Reformation and one the greatest figures as a disciple of Christ History. After reading the bible for himself, God reveals to him the true nature of God concerning the child of God. He concluded that the Catholic Church was operating in spiritual darkness about the essential teachings of the bible. He spoke out against the Catholic religious acts of the flesh by speaking against the outer garments of the clergymen and priesthood and how their garments could not cover the true intent of the heart. Martin introduced to the world spiritual liberties that are only found in the faith and spirit of Christ. Martin nailed a 90-page letter of reform concerning the corrupt practice of selling indulgences to absolve sin. After nailing his letter of discontentment and rebuke to the doors of the Catholic Church, church officials excommunicated him and labeled him a heretic. Nicodemus, a highly influential religious figure, believed, like Catholic clergy, that his own actions ensured his righteousness before God. A study of the scriptures shows why religion has damaged Christianity more than it has helped. The religious idea of man is the denial of the freedom of God's salvation plan for man, which is freely given to anyone who would receive it based on faith and not works. Religion creates barriers and strongholds on the human mind that create a spirit of fear that keeps the human spirit from obtaining the freedom of Christ. Although there should be discipline and self-control in the body of Christ, there is also a spiritual redeeming process that seals every believer unto the full day redemption. Being born again is more than accepting Christ and going to church. It is a lifelong commitment of faith that reconnects you back to the eternal power of God to carry out his will on earth as it is in heaven. The eternal source of God creates eternal life for all humans based on his love and not contentious thoughts of man. The misconception of religion has only caused controversial arguments and debates over the word of God. Many new converts believe it is next to impossible to please the very God who created them, so many people shy away from the faith and never experience spiritual growth.

The freedom of being born again is a priceless jewel that any tangible thing can never replace in this world or the world to come. The cost that was paid to redeem the lost soul of man is a continual flow of power that keeps the believers even during the worst and harsh conditions of human life. To truly taste the salvation plan of God will keep the practitioner of the faith under all distress and trials with the power of writing, speaking, meditating, and hearing the word of God as a power source under all distress or various trials. In the gospel of John, Christ refers to his power as a spiritual drink of water that gives the believer the ability to never thirst again. Spiritual rebirth is the open identification of the water baptism that demonstrates to the world that you are dying to the flesh and living in the spirit. Baptism is not a requirement of salvation, as some believe, but your testimony acknowledges that you have identified with the death and burial of Christ as a believer of the faith. There are also the two symbolical baptisms of the scripture; one of the Old Testament of Israel passing through the Red Sea, and the other New Testament symbol of the blood and water that came steaming down out of the body of Christ when they pierced him in his side on the cross of Calvary. One of the thieves believed Christ was the Messiah, and Christ granted him a place in paradise based on his belief, even though he was not physically baptized. Romans 10:9 is the key and foundation to salvation. Humanity's dual nature is why comprehending God's kingdom is so complex. The spirit nature is the eternal likeness of God, and his physical nature is unto the likeness of his flesh, giving mankind a dual thought process of subconscious and conscious mind. Paul describes the dual nature as a conflict between the new man and the old man. (Galatian 5:17) The warfare of the dual psyche can easily ensnare people by religious propaganda biases or misleading information used to promote a particular mindset or point of view. In fact, there is no boundary within the spirit realm of the almighty God. Although there will be times of persecution, the scripture says if it takes the spirit to redeem you, then it's going to take the spirit to keep you, so don't fear external distraction, thinking you can lose your salvation. (Galatians 1-3) There's nothing you can do to earn salvation, and there is nothing you can do to lose salvation because it's the free gift of God given by faith. A true believer in God is unequivocally characterized by a yearning for God's word. It's alarming how

Spiritual Dyslexia

many Christians avoid the Bible, and most religions rely on unverified biblical concepts. The difference between the two behavior patterns is the religious mindset thinks of itself as right standing with God while looking down on others. A sinner saved by grace mindset recognizes the shortcomings of the flesh as we confess sins daily concerning the flesh. Then there is the once you repent of known sin, you should never commit that sin again, which is another form of religious teaching that sounds good to the ear, but there is no assured guarantee in the flesh. Romans 7: 14-21 Paul writes: For we know that the law is spiritual; but I am carnal, sold under sin. The things I should do, I do not, and the things I should not do, that I do. When I consciously know that I'm doing wrong, it shows that I understand the law, which is good. when I understand my action is wrong, then I should identify with the presence of sin. I then realized that it is no longer I who walks after the flesh, but it is the sin in my life that causes me to fall short. Paul confessed that his physical nature was incapable of goodness; while he knew what was right, he could not act accordingly. Paul speaks to born-again believers about the common internal battles all believers face.

The distinctive writing style of the Gospel of John differs from that of Matthew, Mark, and Luke. Matthew's book strongly references God's spiritual and physical kingdom. Mark wrote the first gospel and persuasively described Christ's spiritual and physical servanthood. The book of Luke highlights the spiritual and physical healings of God, while the book of John focuses on the supernatural realm of the eternal light of God. John's writings reveal three important points. The first point is that Christ is engaged directly with the people's questions about the physical world and the spiritual world to come. His second point challenges mankind's logical understanding through God's supernatural knowledge, leading to enlightenment. The third point is he reveals himself as the Great I AM who spoke with Moses in Exodus 3:14. The fourth Gospel is mainly the same story that shows the universal workings of God told by four different witnesses. There is a noticeable difference in the book of John, which differs from the other three gospels. Christ uses personal issues of life to teach valuable spiritual lessons of salvation. When Christ met the woman at the well, he used his physical thirst to lead to a conversation about the living water of God. After he told her who he was, she became the first gentile convert and witness of God. One of the most compelling facts about Christ's conversation with the Samaritan woman was his ability to know the woman as God knew her. The underlying message of the story about the woman at the well teaches us the power of salvation through justification. Every born-again believer must first make a confession of sin to receive the salvation plan of God. Christ used the miracle of the feeding of the 5000 to teach his disciples that he was the bread of life, which was a direct connection of the Passover to the Holy Communion. Christ teaches Nicodemus that man must be born again to teach him salvation comes from God and not by the works of human flesh. Nicodemus said you are a teacher sent by God because no man can do these miracles except God be with him. Nicodemus viewed the miracles as a sign. The woman at the well said unto Christ, I perceive you are a prophet, so she referred to his prophetic words as a sign that he was the Christ. The man at the pool of Bethesda took up his bed and walked as a sign that Jesus was a healer. John's Gospel, unlike the other three, directly aims to help readers understand Christ's divine nature in human form.

John's gospel imparts spiritual wisdom about salvation—trusting Jesus Christ's atoning sacrifice for humanity's sins. Finally, the Gospel of John grants satisfaction with the eternal expectation of our sin debt being paid in full. After feeding the 5000, Christ told the multitude you seek me because of the miracles, but you should seek after me because I am the bread of life, and whoever eats of me shall never hunger again. Jesus again points to the miracle as a sign that our spiritual need is greater than our physical need. The book of John is the only book that notes Jesus' first public miracle at a wedding feast in Cana, where he turned water into wine. Jesus' mother saw that there was no more wine, so she asked Jesus to meet a physical need to make more wine, and his response was his time had not yet come. It's a common practice of the flesh to be concerned with the physical needs of our day-to-day lives while overlooking the spiritual needs. The gospel of John shares many benefits for believing in Christ, such as the redeeming power to escape the bowels of eternal damnation of the Lake of Fire. As a born-again believer, our most important mission is making disciples by the authority of Christ. The last thing God wants for any human being is eternity in the lake of fire found in the earth's heart. The heart of the earth is the inter-core of solid balls of metal whose temperatures reach about 11,000f, which is about the same temperature as the sun. Yesuh proclaims victory over hell and death in the book of Revelation, which is the greatest benefit known to man. Yesuh the Christ is the only person on the planet Earth that has testified that he was going into the heart of the Earth. (Reference Matthew 12:40 & Revelation 1:17). Yesui also testifies to Peter, saying you are Peter, and on this rock I shall build my church, and the gates of hell shall not prevail against, and I will give you the keys of the Kingdom of Heaven: and whatever you bound earth will be bound in heaven, and whatever you loose on the earth will be loosed in Heaven, which is the secret to your soul winning mission. Have you ever thought about the power that is granted to every born-again believer to bind things on earth as it is in heaven? The objective of being born again is to walk in a newness of light, expelling darkness all around you.

To truly understand the mission field of God, there is a constant reminder that we should have a great concern for others. We have the power to bind them in prayer rather than ridicule and place blame. There are many imposters of the faith, so you must try the spirit by the spirit. If someone claims to be born again and scorns, mocks, or condemns others unworthy of God, then they have not truly understood the meaning of being born again according to Romans 3:23. All have sinned and have fallen short of the Glory of God. Being born again has nothing to do with human weakness or strengths but all to do with God's love for mankind. Some claim that they possess a certain anointing over others, and it's simply not true. They blow on people; they touch people, and they fall out. They wave coats over people, and the entire congregation passes out as

Spiritual Dyslexia

a sign of God's anointing, but to be honest, this behavior is not found in scripture except in times of demon possession. So be careful who you let lay hands or prophetize over your life. Spiritual warfare is an actual reality for every born-again believer because of your kingdom value. I believe that born-again believers can possess the special power of healing, but I don't believe in healing being shown to manipulate or entertain crowds, which demonstrates sacrilegious behavior in certain ministries around the world. The question then is sac religion? Sac-religion: having committed the sacrilegious act of placing one's hope on a religious or holy object or image.

The world system, broken and sick with decay, is consumed by the objects we imagine, creating powerful mind control. Paul said that when they knew God, they did not glorify him as God and were not thankful; instead, they became vain in their imaginations, and their foolish hearts were darkened. Professing themselves to be wise became fools. The Book of John is the book of enlightenment, which has the universal power to regenerate a dark heart. Witnesses often saw Christ's miracles as physical enlightenment, though he performed each one for spiritual enlightenment. Christ said a wicked adulteress generation requires a sign! The question then becomes how can we trust in him? The answer is faith. (Hebrew 11:6) Trust is the 33rd virtue of the Tree of Life and is an invisible fruit that comes from the inter-core of the spirit of God. The born-again believer must have a firm belief, reliability, and strength to believe that Christ is the fulfilled salvation plan of God. Christ went to the grave at 33 as a physical act of divinity to demonstrate God's power and genuine spirit and the meaning of trust. In the book of John, God arranged his divine insight into Hebrew and Greek writings into the bible. John 3:33 reads; He that hath received his testimony has set his seal that God is true. This is why every born-again believer must trust in the testimony of Christ for eternal life.

CHAPTER

GODS UNLIMITED RESOURCES!

"For the earth is the Lord's, and the fullness thereof…" —1 Corinthians 10:26

Many believers in Christ have bought into the false perception that believers of Christ should be poor, less fortunate, or underprivileged to fulfill their spiritual obligation. This ideology is largely because of the misinterpretation of the scripture. For example, look at Jesus' first sermon on the mountain titled The Beauties of Life (Matthews 5:3), which reads blessed is the poor in spirit: for theirs is the kingdom of heaven. This scripture passage contains many key components requiring an examination before concluding that Jesus advocates physical poverty for believers, as the text refers to spiritual poverty. Society defines poverty as a lack of sufficient money to live comfortably or normally. There is a story in the bible about a young, rich ruler who asked Christ to become a disciple.

Christ told him to give away his riches and follow him, and, of course, the rich man turned away from Christ. Was Christ's instruction to give away wealth based on the poverty of his followers or on the principle that a man's heart is where his treasure is? Some believe the Bible contradicts itself; however, if Christ intended to impoverish people, this wouldn't be the case. In the Holy Bible, there are no contradictions, and the bible itself has proven to be the infallible word of God just by its publication alone sailing over 100 million copies annually grossing between 450 to 600 million dollars per year without a human author. To fully understand wealth, spiritual awakening must take place. When looking at Matthews 5:3 through the carnal eye, there is no way to see past the physical veil into the supernatural realm. To understand any scripture, you must have clear clairvoyance of the Holy Spirit. We should always begin clear clairvoyance with an enthusiastic approach; this means we must be excited about learning spiritual things and be extremely grateful for what God reveals to us through his spirit as we seek greater understanding. Call on me and I will answer you, and tell you great and mighty things which you do not know. (Jeremiah 33:3), which is the fullness of God's manifestation. For God has revealed it to us through the spirit. For the Spirit searches all things, even the depths of God. (1 Corinthians 2:10).

The born-again believer has a personal seal placed upon their heart and mind that reconnects them back to the original spiritual state of innocence. Spiritual creation preceded physical creation in the case of Adam and Eve. In this state of awareness, they knew no sin; their bodies were immortal and not designed to die. God designed the body to reproduce physically, and at some point, it would undergo a metaphorical cocoon effect, transforming from spiritual-physical energy into illuminating spiritual energy, as Jesus demonstrated on the mountain of transfiguration. Can you imagine yourself as an eternal, dazzling, radiant light full of wisdom that can never die? Transformation: a complete change of form or appearance into a more beautiful or spiritual state. Many people that have had a near-death experience often refer to this glorious light, while having an out-of-body experience. When Jesus was speaking on the mountainside in (Matthew 5:3) could it be likely that he was referring to the detachment of Spiritual and physical state? Being spiritually poor means that we can't attach ourselves to anything in the physical realm because, in time, we will have to leave all physical possessions behind. Could this be the reason Christ said it's harder for a rich man to enter heaven than a camel to go through the eye of a needle? The physical world can produce a lot of baggage that can weigh the spiritual man down. It is next to impossible to be spiritual while casting your cares on the materials of the physical realm of the world. I found 9 infinitive blessings in the book of Matthews 5:3-12 during Christ's first public sermon: The Beauties. The first point of innocence deals with the change from natural to the supernatural. To be (poor in spirit) simply means that you should have a humble spirit, and never become possessed by worldly possessions. It's very sad to say many wealthy people of the world do not, and will not, reference God, because they become so attached to the physical until they trust in physical possessions instead of God. The story of Lazarus and the rich man tells of a rich man who died with a prideful heart, clinging to his worldly possessions.

He walked past Lazarus every day and never thought to stop and help him in any kind of way. Lazarus would beg the rich man to help him daily, but he refused him every day (Luke 12:15). Take heed and beware of covertness: for a man's life consists not in the abundance of things which he possesses. A man's lips can draw near to Christ, but his heart can be far from Christ. Truly spiritual pride and ignorance are very dangerous and destructive and are one of the worst forms of sin known to man. So Jesus begins his sermon with this message directly to the spirit of a person and not the wealth of a person.

The second point of witness deals with the heart of (people that morn) for society. We live in a fallen society and just as Jesus wept over Jerusalem, things are happening in the world that will cause us to mourn. A narcissistic psychological mindset plagues America, leading to social disorder in all three branches of government: the Legislative, which makes laws; the Executive, whose elected officials uphold and carry out laws; and the Judicial, which evaluates and enforces the law. Therefore, the word of God teaches the believer to pray for its governing power. Jesus' mission was never to overthrow the governing power of the Romans, although many people of that time wanted freedom from the struggles and harsh treatment of Rome. It's a very sad reality when a person can live in a world full of evil, and destruction with no care or concern for other people who are suffering great deals of loss, and just go along with day-to-day life as if they are exempt from the troubles of the world. Jesus comforts those mourning the world's suffering, assuring them that his coming kingdom will establish a society free from evil forever. The third point of manifestation is to focus on the relationship of human beings and how we treat one another.

(A meek person will have peace with God) and get favor with man. Christ is encouraging the believer to treat people as they want to be treated. A positive attitude invites both earthly and heavenly blessings. The fourth point on universal understanding discusses the psychological thought patterns that imprint themselves on the hearts and minds of those Christ has redeemed. When spiritual rebirth takes place, there is a great desire that ignites from within the spirit that supernaturally connects you to the universe all around you. The fifth point is a command to (God shall fill that hunger and thirst for righteousness). The scripture confirms this filling in the book of John in the 4th chapter and 14th verse when Jesus speaks to the woman at the well concerning the human and spiritual thirst. Jesus, in his sermon, describes this thirst as the inner force that draws us toward our God-given purpose or as the negative tension we feel when pulled out of balance toward the works of the flesh. Addressing the Samaritan woman's five husbands, Jesus reveals she was never truly married to any of them. Because Jesus is the righteousness of God, he went to the Samaritan well while the disciples went to buy meat. There of two examples of the true meaning of thirsting and hungering for righteous sake. In the supernatural, we see Jesus focus on the water, which is a type of Holy Spirit, while the disciples focus on the meat, which is a type of flesh. When Jesus originally sent the disciples into the mission field, he told the disciples not to go to Samaria, but the time had arrived for the righteousness of God to be drawn out, and given to all that thirst, even a nation of people that walk after idols. Jews despised Samaritans because of their intermarriages; Jews and Samaritans had no dealings with each other, a fact the woman at the well quickly reminded Jesus of. The living water filled the woman, and she became Samaria's first spiritual convert. The woman quenched her thirst and entered the city, proclaiming her fullness to the men.

Frequently, critics of the faith haven't personally experienced its benefits. God's word is a spring of living water, endlessly satisfying and eternally sufficient. The disciples prayed Christ would eat meat, but he refused and said that he had meat that they did not know about, which is the word and will of God. The sixth point of grace in Christ's sermon on the mountain deals with the behavior of the kingdom mindset of the poor in spirit, and (a merciful heart). Christ teaches us that God's unlimited resources directly connect to our mercy and grace toward others. We learn valuable lessons about forgiveness from the scriptures, enabling us to receive forgiveness. Our normal human thought process trains us to believe people are expendable, so we forget God's mercy and, in turn, withhold mercy from others. The book of Matthew 18:21-35 recounts the greatest story of mercy and forgiveness. The lesson begins with Peter asking concerning the limits of forgiveness, thinking seven times of forgiveness is complete; so that should be good enough. Peter's limited view of forgiveness prevented him from understanding that he would soon require far more forgiveness than someone who had failed many more times. Especially knowing that Christ said; if you deny me before man, I will deny you before the Father. Mercy is always a powerful mindset, because you may never know when you're going to need mercy. Peter received a cryptic communication from Jesus, advising him to forgive 7 times 70 as a symbolic gesture of redemption for Israel's disobedience. Jesus tells his disciples about a man who owed a great debt and out of piety the king forgave his debt, but this same man went to a fellow servant and put his hands around his throat because he owed him a small debt. This man's lack of compassion for his friend's small debt, despite his recent forgiveness of an enormous debt by the king, revealed his corrupt mind. Upon learning of his servant's unforgiveness, the king immediately summoned the servant and gave him to the tormentors for punishment until his debts were paid. Therefore, it is very important to understand the difference between a relationship with God and having the religion of men. Christ would often confront the religious people of his time by calling them the seed of the devil because they were so unmerciful. The believer must always remember that God's mercy is unconditional. Christ's seventh complete point deals with the emotion of the believer being (pure at heart) with righteous motivates and deeds. You receive God's genuine spirit when your emotions are intact. If you notice, he said his burdens were light, not lite! The power of light stimulates sight and makes things visible, even when things are invisible. For centuries, people interpreted this scripture from a single point of view despite its twofold meaning. We overlook the spelling of the word light and interpret it understanding that Christ said his burdens are lite! The definition of lite by that interpretation, is lacking substance or threat. Christ's statement has a twofold interpretation that deals with the spirit and physical makeup of the burdens of man. The emotion of the believer will determine if the believer has light to see during a dark situation. If you are an emotional wreck, you cannot help yourself or anyone else during stormy seasons. Christ uses the illustration of a yoke as a constant reminder that where two or three are gathering in his name; he promises to be in the midst. A yoke tied two oxen together to plow the field, a common farming tool. Yoking two oxen together removed the emotional stress of one ox plowing. The Bible says that two are always better than one because if one falls in a ditch, there is one to help pull him out.

The scripture also warns us against the dangers of being unequally yoked with an unbeliever. The unbeliever lacks the understanding and enlightenment to help you during times of distress, which will cause you to become emotionally drained. Christ was a very emotional teacher who wept for the people, and Jerusalem was an open sign that a true convert soul would often show emotions for others for the mission, faith, and people of God. John 11:35. Jesus wept! The eighth point and new order of Christ's sermon show a biological change in the life of a believer that transfers you into a peacemaker. Peace doesn't come easily in times of storms, but it doesn't mean that peace is unobtainable. A child of God should be a servant to all and envious of no one, which produces an inner peace that surpasses all understanding. A believer's strength, paradoxically stated in the Bible, stems from their weakness. Not by might or by power, but by my spirit, says the Lord Almighty. Zechariah 4:6. Be humble in the presence of God's mighty power, and he will honor you when the time comes. Remember, God cares for you, so turn all your worries over to him. The peacemaker must be able to possess the freedom of thought from the strongholds and mind traps of the enemy.

The ninth and infinite point of Christ's sermon on the mountain deals with the persecutions of the righteous. God guarantees that a persecuted child of God will inherit the Kingdom of Heaven. This inheritance is based on a metaphysic promise that surpasses all principles concerning the gospels, including abstract concepts such as being, knowing, cause, identity time, and space. God granted this metaphysical promise to the thief on the cross after his plea for righteousness. As believers, we know we will suffer for the gospel, but we also have the heavenly assurance of reward when we face hostility and ill-treatment. The cruel death on the cross ended Christ's physical life, but the resurrection of his spirit life destroyed death once and for all. The metaphysic power of God is in Christ, and in Christ, we have the same power over death.

These are the nine points of Christ's Sermon on the Mount. If you apply these nine points of Christ's sermon to your daily walk with God, you will have the kingdom of God in heaven and on earth. Of course, many will disagree with my interpretation, which is ok, but poverty-stricken mindsets will forfeit the opportunity to walk in the fullness of God's blessings. Their hard hearts and stiff necks will cause them to use a legalist approach towards people whom God has promised to give an abundant life. These Christians can be very vicious in their attacks on believers who are prosperous, successful in material terms, and flourishing financially. Giving a tenth of your earnings, or tithing is the primer that releases the flow of God's blessing unto the believer because tithing is 100% a spiritual activation system that opens up the windows of heaven causing blessing that overflows in the spirit, and physical life of the believer. (Malachi 3:10) Never should anyone tithe out of greed or selfish motives for material gain; many have tried to manipulate the system but failed. To connect to walk in the blessing's fullness of God, the believer must be intentional, directional, purposeful, and thankful in their spiritual approach to GOD. The believer must be able to see beyond human reasoning by reprogramming the neurosensory of the brain with the word of God, which will maximize your full potential in receiving the fullness of the blessing. By divine insight, you will discern all things by the spirit of God through foresight, while the world communicates based on hindsight. This type of blessing is based on the favor of God, and not the favor of God, because with God there is no respecter of persons! Don't worry about doing good; God's resources are endless, and you will reap a harvest in His time. (Acts 10:3)

 The trick of the devil is to blind the imagination because we are living on enemy-occupied territory and the force of darkness has come to kill, steal, and destroy. Satan's goal is to cause mankind to be bound by the stronghold of pessimism. Pessimistic people tend to see the worst aspect of things or believe that the worst will happen with a lack of hope for the future. The pessimist-thinking individual always looks for the downside of life while overlooking all the beauty that life offers. When a pessimistic person reads the bible, they never seem to see God for his love and grace, because they only focus on the wrath of God. Wisdom teaches a valuable lesson in the book of Proverbs that speaks expressly concerning the unlimited riches of God, which are available to all who seek him, including eternal life. Pessimist Christians do not have full assurance in anything, not even their soul's salvation, so they can't share the gospel of salvation. The pessimist, despite having donated nothing to the church, always complains extensively about its finances. While many scriptures mention abundant life's riches and treasures, true abundance isn't just about material possessions; owning a Porsche doesn't make you its manufacturer. Despite material abundance, many lack a spiritual connection to Christ, leading to miserable lives. (Luke 12:25) The earth belongs to the Lord, yet since humanity's fall, God's enemy has controlled it. Christ, however, already redeemed it spiritually and will physically redeem it upon the fulfillment of all things. The believer can experience victory while living in the worldly system of the enmity. When people like Judas try to use or manipulate God out of blessings; that person has just signed his or her death warrant, as with Ananias and Sapphire when they lied to the Holy Spirit. (Acts 5: 1-10) Although there is no such thing as a prosperity gospel; the gospel will cause you to prosper. Seeking God for material gain and worldly wealth is the total opposite of seeking God with the right heart and mind. (Colossians 1:12-20) Give thanks to God our Father, who has enabled us to receive the inheritance of the saints in the light! An inheritance is an object or class based on another object or class using the same implementation to maintain the same behavior patterns and rights of the estate. God has delivered us from the power of darkness and has transferred us into the kingdom of light, which is only found in Christ Jesus in whom we have redemption through his blood, even the forgiveness of sin. Jesus, the exact representation of the invisible God and the firstborn of all creation, is the seed of all things, heavenly and earthly, visible and invisible, including thrones, dominions, rulers, and authorities—he created all things through himself and for himself. Christ is before all things, and by him, all things exist. As Christ leads the church, its members, and his body, are the first to rise from the dead.

The process of reconciliation gave the peace that surpasses us through the blood of the cross, whether it is things in the heavens or things on the earth with an unlimited supply of grace and mercy. Believers often struggle to grasp the concept of material loss. It is quite normal for believers to experience the stress of emotional detachment when dealing with death, loss of jobs, divorce, foreclosure, sickness, or any other physical distress of the normal cycles of life, whether good or bad. In the scripture, these uncertain times are called seasons. All humans will go through different seasons in life as a trying of the faith. Unless we face trials that test our faith, how can we learn to truly trust God and discover our resilience? There is a significant difference between going through a season or trial and operating outside of the will of God. Some people are not in a season of testing, but are living in open rebellion! The Bible refers to this type of mindset as stiffed necked. The true believer must become trained by the word of God to recognize and understand how to encounter each season we face in life by depending totally on God. Personally, as I write this chapter of this book, I'm dealing with the experience of being laid off for the first time in my life at 42. Of course, I think about the lost

Spiritual Dyslexia

resources that the job has provided for me all of those years of my employment while dealing with the fact that this company has found reasons to deny unemployment claims. How do I overcome my current situation? To be frank, I've announced my intention to exit the industrial gas industry within two years because of its demanding and hazardous nature. After ten years of working as a delivery driver, the workload took its toll on my body, and it showed. I see the termination as a blessing, and a sense of relief because it would be days I handled physically, loading and unloading over ten thousand pounds of hazardous steel. Once you have experience in the industrial gas business, your experience will create other opportunities for you. Although I made a lot of connections over the years, it was just time for me to get out of the business. By aligning my thoughts with the universe, I landed an interview for my dream job the day after I stopped focusing on it. Christ is the greatest teacher, and his teachings are the direct interconnections between his spirit and our spirit. If you think that God's resources have limits, then the resources in your life will have limits. The worst place you want to be as a child of God is a space of limits. You must continue to remind yourself the earth is the Lord and the fullness thereof, and he shall supply all of your needs according to the riches in the glory of Christ Jesus. (Philippians 4:19) 4=universe 1= God 9=infinity. The universal God is infinite! Another important key to understanding the unlimited resources of God deals with the exhortation of others over oneself. The endless recourses of God will never end, because God is always giving of himself on behalf of us while communicating his will emphatically through his word. A sure way to shorten your blessings is to talk negatively on the behalf of someone else blessings. The recourses of God are a reciprocating force and we should encourage and build one another up so we can flow in the power of God.

It's a known fact that when we speak ill of others, we risk cutting off the flow of God's power and unlimited resources in our own lives. There is an old helm that said: You can't beat God-given, no matter how hard you try! The more you give; the more he gives to you, so just keep on giving, because it's true! Jesus said if you don't believe my word, then believe my works. In other words, you will be able to tell a tree by the fruit it bears. Every ministry does not have God's best interest at hand, so remember, big doesn't always mean better. Each believer has the sole responsibility of trying the spirit by the spirit of God, and you will discern if you're dealing with a genuine spirit of God or a spirit of manipulation. Please don't become blinded by Satan's mind trap of the false idea that all spiritual leaders with unlimited resources are not of God. Scripture shows that, according to the promises to Abraham, God would bless all families, both those born into the family and those adopted. Abraham's vast wealth led to powerful and wealthy descendants who established mighty kingdoms. So where did the idea originate that the church is supposed to be poor and broke? It originated from the pits of hell based on bad interpretation and misapplication of scripture! Knowing the kingdom's wealth intimately, the devil deceives you, exploiting any opportunity to convince you of your poverty. It takes money to advance the kingdom of God, so if you believe that having money as a child of God is wrong, then you don't understand the cost of kingdom-building.

Spiritual Dyslexia

When King Solomon was building the temple of God, he gave 3,000 tons of gold and 30,000 tons of silver out of the nation's treasury, and I'm pretty sure there were people of that time criticizing the work saying the temple didn't need 22billion dollars, worth of gold in it, and 600 million in silver is just ridiculous! We must remember how we identify with gold and silver as treasure differs from God because all gold, silver, diamonds, and precious are building materials that all belong to God. Although we should value money as a good steward, we must never forget money is just a government mint or tool for trade. So many people are against the idea of mega-churches, forgetting the fact that every time Jesus spoke, he drew mega crowds of 4 to 5 thousand people that he also fed unlimited resources. A resource, as we'll define it, comprises the financial, material, personnel, and other assets used by individuals, organizations, or organisms for effective functioning. The world widely accepts this definition as a rule of thumb for all companies except the Church, which is the only Christ-conscious institution on Earth. It seems to be an objective plan to disrupt the advancement of the kingdom of God on planet earth, and many professing Christians agree with the worldview of a finical strong Church. I've seen interviews by one of the world's greatest rappers talking against the church, and its financial operation, while he spent millions of dollars on jewelry, clothes, cars, parties, and homes, and died broke leaving no inheritance for his future generation, and many people of the world today would label him as one of the greatest conscious leaders of our time. (TUPAC)

The devil is so crafty he is now working in the minds of men and women in government seats to implement taxes on the

Church because she has made a global impact financially, even though demons thought they would stump her out through persecution. We achieve abundant living only when we retrain our hearts from worldly things to Godly things, a process impossible through human effort alone, as the dangers of pride will unexpectedly arise. Committing 100% to trusting Christ enables you to address shortcomings; therefore, repent swiftly and maintain your trust in Christ. With a repentant heart, God's will takes precedence. His spirit supports your faith-filled path and, thus, doesn't depend on what you see. We must become fully persuaded to know that dishonoring God is the root cause of all sin. God's word states He considers the body His temple and will honor what was sown in dishonor. Be free to confess it all to God, because he knows anyway. Recognizing that you were bought at a price helps you understand your value and worth. Certain things you will not want to do, while there will be other things that you will battle with not doing because of the stain of sin. Hang in there, because it is all a part of the scarification process that comes with the renewing of the mind. Seek the word of God with a conscious effort and not conform to the ways of the world. Many people don't understand this process, so they give up on the faith saying it's too hard, thinking they can win God's approval with acts of the flesh, which is impossible and a waste of time. When you think about being set aside for the master's use, it will always bring honor to God as well as yourself, so stay focused on God. The importance of prayer and supplication lies in their ability to help you communicate with and address your inner struggles.

Spiritual Dyslexia

Many Christians mistakenly believe that God works like Santa Claus, granting wishes from a list, leading to disappointment when prayers go unanswered. When seeking an abundant life, we must abstain from all manners of sexual perversion which will lead our heart to diversion of the truth. God's word will enlighten your subconscious, granting access to limitless resources when you consciously engage with it through hearing and reading. This abundant life is then yours.

CHAPTER

7

THE SEVEN CHURCHES OF REVELATION

In the book of Revelation, John the Beloved makes his salutation to the Seven Churches and Seven Spirits, which are before the throne of Christ. In the seven dispensations of time, there are two ages in which the angels ministered to mankind before Christ, and there are two ages when angels ministered to man after Christ. Jesus stood in the middle of these two ages for 33 years, ministering and unveiling his bride, the Church. The book says, "Here I am; I come, as it is written about me." Psalms 40: 7, which can be interpreted as 4=universal & 7= complete. Each age comprises a past, present, and future. The first age is the Original Earth, the Dark Formless Void Earth, and the Restored Earth. The second age is the Fall of Man, The Flood, and the Tower of Babel, unto the time of the dedication of King Solomon's temple. Between the first and second ages, you have the birth, death, and resurrection of the long-awaited Messiah. He revealed his second coming, his Church, the Rapture, and Tribulation Ages. This is then followed by his second coming.

The two ages that follow his second coming comprise Israel restored as God's chosen nation, the Armageddon war, and Satan bounded for a thousand years. The last age comprises the Millennium Valley, the Earth restored by fire, and the New Earth. These are the prophetic mysteries of the seven golden candlesticks that John saw in his vision. "And I turned to see the voice that spake with me. And being turned, I saw seven golden candlesticks; And in the midst of the seven candlesticks one like unto the Son of man, clothed with a garment down to the foot, and girt about the paps with a golden girdle." Revelation 1:12-13. The book of Exodus 25:31-40 reveals the mystery of the candlestick through Moses' menorah. The menorah is the illuminating light of divine understanding, which enlightens the human mind concerning the word and will of God. John's vision shows Christ standing among the branches of the menorah, revealing his enlightening word to dispel John's darkness. The menorah was first given to Moses as a symbolic symbol that communicates God's present and handy work throughout the history of mankind as a supernatural guide light by his spoken word, which is the manifestation of Christ as Moses talked to him in Mt. Sinai while receiving the blueprints for the menorah.

The design's detailed instructions are the Holy Spirit's guiding light for born-again believers. Solid gold symbolizes God's purity, his self-refinement, and indestructible nature, constantly illuminating humanity's spirit, soul, and body with its radiant light in a dark world. The menorah is the revelation of Christ

Spiritual Dyslexia

sharing his glory with man. The Spirit of God, revealing all things of God, even the deep things, is given to those who embrace Christ. (1 Corinthians 2:10). Jesus shared his glory with humanity so believers could reflect his image to the world. If there is no reflection of his image in the life of a believer, then we bring him to open shame. (John 1.) In the beginning was the Word, and the Word was with God, and the Word was God. Revelation 19:16 tells us who is the Christ and what his name is.

John's letters addressed seven churches; however, only one church was affected by seven spirits, symbolizing the conduct of its members within God's universal church. John's letter is a written testimony of the witness of Christ present within the body of the Church and writes his observation. It is very important to note that Revelation is not the last book of the bible but the blueprint to the whole Bible's schematics, legends, and pictorial gram, with Christ as the master designer.

According to the bylaws of the Church, I've been spiritually ordained by God for the purpose of all things being done decently and in order. (1 Corinthians 14:40) There are seven short-form golden rules that every Church should operate by to fulfill the spiritual laws of Christ. First of all, the church should promote and communicate effectively the will of God and his universal covenant plan of salvation. Second, the Church should provide directions and articulate its mission and responsibility to seek the lost souls of humanity with the focus of grace to all who seek to be saved. Third, the church must preserve the unity and bond of peace within the body of believers by standing in faith and trusting in the testimony of Christ. Fourth, the Church should be a place of protection and should make sure that all of its members are operating in the same spirit of God before they are to perform or fill any role of leadership in the Church. Fifth, God appoints the church pastor, and the pastor elects the elders, deacons, missionaries, and laymen after they humbly prove themselves worthy of their calling. Sixth, the Church should always operate with Grace being the abiding rule of faith, never deviating from the word of God. Seventh, the Church should always have an active plan of fellowship as a key component as a governing body of believers with a heart and mind that tends to the needs of others with a spirit to restore those who may fall by the wayside during a time of testing.

John's revelation of the seven churches holds historical significance for humanity and world history; Christ first mentioned the church to Peter, saying, "On this rock I will build my church." The angelical message was given to John telling the spiritual story of a mortal man and his journey in life with divine insight into the universal Church of Christ.

In the book of Revelation, John was enlightened with angelical information to unlock the mysteries of man and his union with his creator. The first star, and spiritual message to the physical church of Ephesus is connected by the Euphrates

Spiritual Dyslexia

River, which was first mentioned in the 14th verse of Genesis. The river is in the Garden of Eden, where the Lord God placed man. Whenever the scripture references the Lord God, it's a direct connection to the presence of Christ living in the spiritual realm before he was physically born. Christ is the physical image of God, and God made man in that image. This initial message to the Ephesians unlocks a communication code, showing us that the spiritual church existed eternally before its physical form appeared in the New Testament. Although there is no direct connection in history that reveals the manifestation of the church, there is a strong reference found in the ancient historical manuscript. The modern church is the prophecy from the ancient writings of Enoch and her successful stages of spiritual maturity through a personal relationship with God. Christ addresses their patience, labor, and focus based on their kingdom work, and he addresses their lack of spiritual growth. Christ commends them for their efforts of righteousness and their devotion but confronts their backslidden ways concerning their first love. Many churches start with a great zeal for Christ and then get sidetracked with the business of the church and become self-dependent. Adam leaves his first love and provides for himself by sewing fig leaves together. The connection of the church should never become disconnected from Christ. The physical church of Ephesus had become perverse during its time of persecution they turned from God. Many false apostles emerged in the Ephesus church, and while Christ praised those who stood up for his name, he strongly rebuked the church of Ephesus for relying too much on themselves. Christ warns the church about its sinful condition, urging repentance and a return to their original devotion, or face expulsion and the removal of their candlestick. Christ confronts the church for taking on a worldly spirit like the proselyte Nicolas, which is a type of religious act of the flesh comingling with the world occultism and pagan practices within the church. Things like Easter egg hunts, Christmas trees, and the Halloween Day of Evil. The entire pagan rituals are deemed as harmless fun! This is the same Spirit of Nicolaitanes, which Christ hates. He that has an ear let them hear what the Spirit said unto the churches; to him that overcomes I will give to eat from the tree of life, which connects us to the tree of life, and the Garden of Eden (Paradise).

The second star and spiritual message to the physical church of Smyrna connect us to a time and space encompassing all the physical suffering of mortal man from Adam to the resurrected Christ. God promised Abraham's believing descendants that the Messiah would be sacrificed for the world's sins; however, some who claim to be Abraham's descendants rejected Christ and refused to accept him as the Messiah. Christ reminds them of the tribulation and poverty, as well as the blessings that would follow them as the promised seed to Abraham. The ten days of tribulation could mean the increment of how we calculate years into decades, centuries, and millenniums concerning all tribulations that the Hebrew and Gentile people have suffered and will suffer. The angelic message to the Smyrna Church covers the Spiritual Dispensation of Promise. This was the promise that was first given to Abraham for his faith to follow the eternal God of the universe. Abraham believed God, and God accounted it to him as righteousness. Therefore, God promised Abraham he would become the father of a great nation. After many years of testing and trials, God gave Abraham a new promise: he would become the father of all nations. Christ confronts their ideology that supports the breaking of God's established Law of Moses. The church operated fully for worldly and political power, which is spoken of as the seat of Satan. Unable to destroy the church, Satan influenced its members to exalt it with false motives, mirroring the Israelites' worship of the golden calf while Moses received the Ten Commandments on Mount Sinai. Constantine's political power and governing laws, motivated by Balaam's spirit, led to the fusion of church and state, resulting in idolatry. Removing God's laws and implementing a new doctrine with emperors, popes, and clergymen, Roman authorities established a new institution of power. This new institution grafted Christianity and pagan influences together, merging the Roman Empire and creating the Papal Church. According to Acts 20:7, the Christian church gathered on the first day of the week (Sunday), after the Sabbath Rest, to preach the Gospel of Jesus Christ and partake in the Lord's supper, which was coded in the Laws of Moses as the first fruit offering on the eighth day. As a sun worshipper, Constantine saw a great political opportunity to further his power and influence by signing into law Sunday as Sabbath, seeing that great multitudes of people, or the church, were already gathering to hear the preached resurrected word of Christ while giving God the first fruit praise and worship on the 8th day. Often, God has used the plans of the enemy to carry out his own plans, which introduce and establish what is known as the bride of Christ: the church. Before Constantine's Roman legal system, the church had a long-standing tradition of gathering on the first day of the week, its origins tracing back to the Holy Spirit's arrival. Peter preached the word of God with a cloven tongue as men from all over the world understood him in their language. As it is written, if Satan had known what he was doing when he crucified the Lord, he would have never crucified him. (1 Corinthians 2: 8) It's a noted fact that the Sabbath is the day of rest, and Sunday is the day of worship. These are two distinct orders of operation, and one day has not taken the place of the other. Refer to the Leviticus Law on the 7th day of Sabbath and the 8th day of the first fruit offering. (Leviticus 9: 1-7, 23:14-19) We must remember that the Sabbath was a day of rest, and the priest did the only work that was permitted in the temple on Sabbath sacrifice. The Church is not a temple or a building but the gathering of two or more people agreeing in the name of Christ. The Sabbath is a gift of rest from God to man, and Sunday is the gift of praise and worship from man to God.

God rewards His faithful, deceased saints with the crown of life, a prize earned throughout history. Christ wears this crown and shares it with all those who fought the good fight of faith unto death. Those who refused the mark of the beast were killed, and those Old Testament saints who refused to break God's law and bow to Babel were killed and tormented. During Satan's release from his thousand-year imprisonment, many saints' spirits will rise. Christ resurrected and redeemed the slain spirits and souls of the Church; therefore, they will not be harmed, and eternal death will be granted to all who opposed God's Law. Revelation 20:4-15

The third star and spiritual message to the physical church of Pergamos continued in the spirit of Balaam, which also violates the nullification of God's Law. Even though they were professor of the faith, they behaved in the spiritual likeness of the children of Israel when they worshipped false gods. God's law is demonstrated in three phases within the spirit of these three churches. God first gave the Law, then it was broken, and now Christ has nullified the Law. The Spirit of the church of Pergamos was not only responsible for breaking God's Law; they also went as far as establishing their own pagan laws within the Church. Christ grants them the opportunity to repent for engaging in immoral behavior, mirroring the actions of the Israelite men who partook in the sensuous revelry with Moabite women. The Pergamos Church held onto the name of Christ, but this did not give them the right to pollute the grace of God by creating a false sense of grace.

The fourth star and spiritual message to the physical church of Thyatira was also guilty of the same acts of disobedience of the former two churches in the breaking of God's law and allowing the false doctrine of the spirit of Jezebel to be taught within the church which is a direct connection to a time in history when Jezebel the false prophetess married Ahab the 7th King of Israel, causing him to abandon the worship of God and encourage false worship of the deities Baal and Asherah. Although the church did great works of charity, they allowed this pretender of the faith to seduce them with acts of fornication and sacrifices to idol gods. This is how the Papal Church influenced people to bow before statues and images created by the hands of man while teaching the people that the Papal Church is superior to the word of God, which speaks the opposite of God's Law.

The fifth star and spiritual message to the physical church of Sardis are identified as the dead church. Though its name meant "alive," this church's ritualistic worship had become so formal that only the form of God remained. The spirit of this church also connects us back to Enoch and his walk with God before he was raptured out as he prophesied about a people in time that would be called out before the great dreadful day of tribulation. Christ identifies those justified by faith, sealed for redemption's day, and clothed in white—symbolizing the Lamb's wedding feast—because they followed God's commandments.

―――――――・♦♦♦♦・―――――――

The sixth star's message reveals Philadelphia's physical church as a church of brotherly love, mirroring Sardis' graceful and loving nature. They carried out the will of God in the adoption of the gentile nation who came to Christ. The spirit of revival had branched out of the weakness of the Sardis Church. By rejecting Christ's work on the cross, many false Jews denied the Gentiles' engraftment into God's New Nation. Christ testifies of himself and his seat on the throne of David and sets up an open door of fellowship to whoever will come. This proclamation of Christ connects us directly to a time in the gospels when Jesus gave the parable about the wedding feast and the invitation to God's grace. This church included Messianic Jews and

Gentile converts who believed Christ was the Father's only son and Israel's redeemer. Christ's prophecy foretells a future New Jerusalem, its gates bearing the names of those who survived attacks from false Jews who killed numerous Jewish Christians. Christ has opened a door that no man can shut, and that is the door of grace.

The seventh star's complete message to the physical church of Laodicea concludes John's vision of the operation of the church periods that continue to operate. Specifically, the Angel's spiritual message is directed toward the Laodicean Church. The Spirit's message condemned every dark spirit of manipulation that sought to exploit God for personal gain and worldly possessions. Christ said the members of the church are lukewarm and good for nothing! The focus of the heart of these people is usury and greed. This message was not condemning the blessing and financial wealth of God's people but was pointing out the fact that there are hirelings and wolves amongst the sheep that think God doesn't see the purpose and intent of their heart to take advantage of an opportunity to get rich quickly. Christ said he stands outside the doors of many of these churches because they have become purely mechanical and formatted by music, entertainment, and self-deception. These egotistic people, known in the church as the great pretenders, use song and dance and persuasion to control the hearts and minds of the people. Although they can fool many unsuspecting victims, God is not deceived. The signs that follow these people of heresies will always deviate from the word of God while focusing on the prosperity of the world. They focus on things for themselves and take pride in the works of their hand, forgetting who gave them the strength to build. They are very self-centered and very subjective thinking people who want to have control over people and are not loyal to the very people who serve them. This abuse of power has destroyed the kingdom, nation, and families, and wants to destroy the Church of God. Christ acknowledges their work but wants them focused on kingdom building; however, their self-absorption prevents them from seeing the need for change. This is the complete message to the seven spirits of the seven golden candlesticks of the seven churches of Asia. Revelation 1:1-20, and 3:1-21. He that hath an ear let them hear.

ABOUT THE AUTHOR

Duane Curtis McDermott
A Journey of Faith, Redemption, and Creativity

I was born on February 15, 1974, in Houston, Texas, to my loving parents, Meva and Paul McDermott. Though our upbringing was modest, it was rich in values—respect, integrity, and morality—anchored by the golden rule: *treat others as you wish to be treated.*

As the middle child between two brothers, I often struggled to find my own identity. After my parents' divorce, I veered off course, searching for direction in all the wrong places. Unlike my brothers, who graduated from high school, I became the so-called *black sheep* of the family, dropping out in the tenth grade. But in 1994, determined to rewrite my story, I earned my GED—scoring exceptionally high on the writing portion. That moment sparked something deep within me. Despite my lifelong battle with dyslexia, I discovered a passion for writing that would later define my purpose.

That same year, my first son, Lil Duane, was born, followed four years later by my daughter, Destyny. Then, 25 years later,

I welcomed my two youngest children, Dorian and Deanna, blessings that reaffirmed my faith in God's perfect timing.

In 1994, still searching for meaning, I visited Mosque Temple #45 in Houston under the leadership of Robert Muhammad. Encouraged by a community acquaintance, Qornell X, I sought structure and discipline. Instead, I left feeling unsettled. The strict security measures, the assigned seating, and the atmosphere of control made me feel less like a guest and more like a suspect. At the end of the meeting, I was handed a card to sign, a declaration stating, *"There is no god but Allah."* Raised in a Christian home, I had only ever known Jesus as my Lord and Savior. Yet, at that moment, I signed the card.

That night, my life changed forever. As I lay in bed, reflecting on what I had done, I heard a voice—calm yet firm—speak directly to my spirit: *"The only God your people ever told you about was the Lord Christ Jesus, and you signed Him away in minutes based on man's words?"* The weight of conviction fell upon me. Overwhelmed, I dropped to my knees in repentance, and in that moment, I felt the undeniable presence of the Almighty. From then on, I rededicated my life to Jesus Christ, rejecting all other paths and embracing my faith with unwavering devotion.

For the past 30 years, I have immersed myself in the study of scripture, enduring trials and triumphs that have strengthened my spiritual walk. Through divine inspiration, I have become a writer of faith-based works, using my pen as a vessel for Christ's message. My self-published books—*The 49 Virtues of Faith, The Whispers of Gabriel,* and *Spiritual Dyslexia*—along with my plays and YouTube short films, stand as testimonies of redemption, faith, and purpose.

Today, I continue to share my story, hoping to inspire others to seek truth, embrace faith, and walk boldly in the grace of Jesus Christ.